# OS X App Development with CloudKit and Swift

Bruce Wade

Apress®

*OS X App Development with CloudKit and Swift*

Bruce Wade
Suite No. 1408, North Vancouver,
British Columbia, Canada

ISBN-13 (pbk): 978-1-4842-1879-2          ISBN-13 (electronic): 978-1-4842-1880-8
DOI 10.1007/978-1-4842-1880-8

Library of Congress Control Number: 2016941345

Managing Director: Welmoed Spahr
Lead Editor: Louise Corrigan
Development Editor: James Markham
Technical Reviewer: Charlie Cruz
Editorial Board: Steve Anglin, Pramila Balen, Louise Corrigan, James DeWolf, Jonathan Gennick,
    Robert Hutchinson, Celestin Suresh John, Nikhil Karkal, Michelle Lowman, James Markham,
    Susan McDermott, Matthew Moodie, Jeffrey Pepper, Douglas Pundick, Ben Renow-Clarke, Gwenan Spearing
Coordinating Editor: Nancy Chen
Copy Editor: April Rondeau
Compositor: SPi Global
Indexer: SPi Global

Distributed to the book trade worldwide by Springer Science+Business Media New York, 233 Spring Street, 6th Floor, New York, NY 10013. Phone 1-800-SPRINGER, fax (201) 348-4505, e-mail orders-ny@springer-sbm.com, or visit www.springer.com. Apress Media, LLC is a California LLC and the sole member (owner) is Springer Science + Business Media Finance Inc (SSBM Finance Inc). SSBM Finance Inc is a Delaware corporation.

For information on translations, please e-mail rights@apress.com, or visit www.apress.com.

Apress and friends of ED books may be purchased in bulk for academic, corporate, or promotional use. eBook versions and licenses are also available for most titles. For more information, reference our Special Bulk Sales–eBook Licensing web page at www.apress.com/bulk-sales.

Any source code or other supplementary materials referenced by the author in this text is available to readers at www.apress.com. For detailed information about how to locate your book's source code, go to www.apress.com/source-code/.

Printed on acid-free paper

# Contents at a Glance

# Contents

# About the Author

**Bruce Wade** is a software engineer from British Columbia, Canada. He started in software development when he was sixteen years old by coding his first website. He went on to study computer information systems at DeVry Institute of Technology in Calgary. To further enhance his skills, he studied visual and game programming at The Art Institute Vancouver. Over the years he has worked for large corporations as well as several startups. His software experience has led him to utilize many different technologies, including C/C++, Python, Objective-C, Swift, Postgres, and JavaScript. In 2012 he started the company Warply Designed to focus on mobile 2D/3D and OS X development. Aside from hacking out new ideas, he enjoys spending time hiking with his boxer Rasco, working out, and exploring new adventures.

# About the Technical Reviewer

**Charles Cruz** is a mobile application developer for the iOS, Windows Phone, and Android platforms. He graduated from Stanford University with B.S. and M.S. degrees in engineering. He lives in Southern California and runs a photography business with his wife (www.bellalentestudios.com). When not doing technical things, he plays lead guitar in an original metal band (www.taintedsociety.com). Charles can be reached at codingandpicking@gmail.com and @CodingNPicking on Twitter.

# Introduction

Over the years, applications have required more and more data that couldn't possibly fit onto a single computer. Not only that, but with mobile devices developers needed to find a way to ensure the same data can be shared between all devices. Apple also saw this need and invented CloudKit, which allows data storage to be infinitely scaled to meet user demand. CloudKit also works across all Apple products, and Apple even recently opened up JavaScript APIs that allow us to develop web applications that access the same data as our desktop, TvOS, and iOS devices.

In this book we are going to work through creating an OS X application from prototype to fully functional, data-driven app using CloudKit. When you are finished with this book you will be able to leverage CloudKit for your own OS X or iOS applications. We will not be covering iOS development in this book; however, the APIs you use for OS X and iOS are identical.

## How This Book Is Organized

### Chapter 1: Introduction

This will provide an overview of this book, what software is required, what you are expected to know, and an overview of what we will be creating.

### Chapter 2: Prototyping Our App

In this chapter we will really start to dive into the planning of our dog parks app. We will primarily be using Sketch 3 in this chapter; however, we will also learn how to use Keynote for basic animations to get a feel for our app before we start coding or even open Xcode.

### Chapter 3: Figuring Out What Data We Need to Store

In this chapter we will take a closer look at our prototype from the previous chapter to dissect what data we really need in order to turn this prototype into a data-driven application. We will also determine which data should be public and which should be private for only your eyes.

### Chapter 4: Introduction to CloudKit

In this chapter we are going to be taking a closer look at CloudKit and how it works. We will cover user authentication, public and private databases, record types, security roles, subscription types, and zones. While we cover these topics we will be taking a closer look at the CloudKit dashboard.

## Chapter 5: Creating Test Data with CloudKit Dashboard

In this chapter we will start adding test data that we will use to display in a working app in subsequent chapters. We will cover how to create public data and how to edit and delete data through the dashboard.

## Chapter 6: Making Our Prototype More Real

Finally, in this chapter we will start migrating our prototype to Xcode so we can have a working app. We will only write enough code to handle authentication and retrieving and displaying our test data in our running app.

## Chapter 7: Updating CloudKit Data from Our App

In chapter 5 we learned how to create/edit/delete data using the CloudKit dashboard. In this chapter we will learn how to update our test data from our app. Then we will implement security roles so users cannot edit data that they have not created themselves.

## Chapter 8: Adding Local Cache to Improve Performance

Finally, in this last chapter we will look at improving performance using a local cache of our data. This will both save server resources and allow the basics of the app to still work, even when there are network connectivity issues.

# CHAPTER 1

# Introduction

We are living in an exciting time in which data-driven applications (DDAs) are becoming an indispensable way of life. Unfortunately, creating a data-driven application isn't always the most straightforward process. When developing DDAs we have to worry about network connectivity, web services, scalability, security, app authentication, performance, and how to handle data synchronization between apps and devices. If this feels like a huge undertaking, you are not alone.

With the release of Apple's CloudKit, most of these concerns have been eliminated to the point where we don't even have to think or know about them. There is no longer a need for a user to enter a username and password (as long as they are logged into iCloud) and Apple handles all scalability issues; there is also no need to write custom web services (this unfortunately has its own limitations). There are a few remaining areas to deal with, including performance, data synchronization, and network connectivity.

Apple has also supplied a web-based dashboard interface, which provides a way to manage an application's data and enables the user to get started as fast as possible. As you will learn in a later chapter, this dashboard makes it extremely simple to manage and monitor your data.

With CloudKit's very generous usage limits there is no better time than now to start building data-driven applications.

## Goals of This book

In this book we are going to work through creating a dog parks OS X application using Swift and CloudKit. Before we jump into coding we will create a basic prototype of our application, to which we will gradually add more functionality until we have a completely functional data-driven application.

## Assumptions about the Reader

To get the most out of this book it is recommended and assumed that you have at least gone through the *Swift Programming Language* book for Swift version 2 provided by Apple. If you have no background knowledge of the Swift programming language you may struggle with some parts of this book.

A fundamental knowledge of OS X development is required, as this book will not be walking you through the basics. If you are new to OS X development you might want to check out *Swift OS X Programming for Absolute Beginners* from Apress.

Finally, you are expected to know how to navigate around OS X, especially the App Store and Safari.

---

**Electronic supplementary material** The online version of this chapter (doi:10.1007/978-1-4842-1880-8_1) contains supplementary material, which is available to authorized users.

# Software Requirements

Over the course of this book we will be using Sketch 3 (free trial or full version), Keynote, Xcode, and the CloudKit dashboard. In this section we will cover downloading the required software.

## Downloading Sketch 3

Sketch 3 is becoming a very popular application for UI design; it can be used for designing mobile, web, and desktop applications. There are a lot of talented designers moving away from Adobe Photoshop and focusing primarily on Sketch 3. The beauty of Sketch 3 is how easy it is to use for designers and developers alike.

We can download Sketch 3 directly from Bohemian Coding. You can either download a trial version or pay for the full version. If you want to save your files to iCloud, make sure you first have iCloud Drive enabled.

1. Open Safari and navigate to `https://www.sketchapp.com`.

2. When the page loads you will be presented with two options:

    a. Free Trial

    b. Buy

3. If you want to just try Sketch 3 (all that is needed for this book), select the "Trial" option. Otherwise, click on "Buy" for an unlimited version.

We will cover the basics of using Sketch 3 later. Also, I will provide a resource for free online videos that will teach you more on how to use Sketch 3.

## Downloading and Installing Keynote

If you purchased your Mac computer in the last few years you should have Keynote installed already. If not, you will have to purchase it from the OS X App Store if you wish to follow along with the Keynote portion of this book.

1. Click on the OS X App Store Icon in the Dock ⬆ .

2. Search for "Keynote."

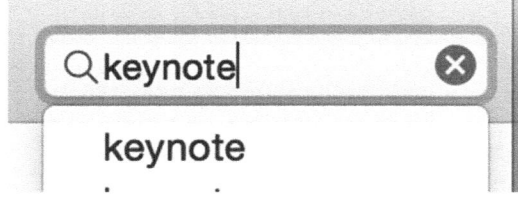

3.  When the search results have loaded, select the Keynote icon to learn more.

**Keynote**
Productivity
★★★☆☆ 8 Ratings
Essentials
OPEN ▾

4.  Select the option to Buy/Install. Mine shows OPEN, as I have already installed Keynote.

# Downloading and Installing Xcode

While Xcode is going to be our most heavily used tool, it is important to resist the urge to jump in and start coding. Diving in is acceptable when you are writing code for testing purposes or trying something from a tutorial you saw online or in a book. However, when you are making a real project you need to start with a prototype, a step that Apple has been emphasizing over the last few years at their development conferences.

Prototyping: Faking It Till You Make It - `https://developer.apple.com/videos/play/wwdc2014-223/`
Designing for the Future Hardware - `https://developer.apple.com/videos/play/wwdc2015-801/`
To download Xcode from the OS X App Store, do the following:

1.  Click on the OS X App Store Icon in the Dock .

2.  Search for "Xcode."

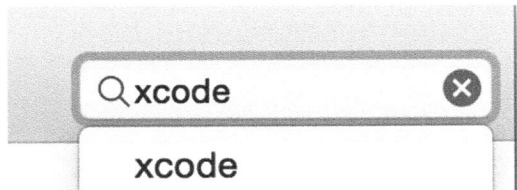

3.  When the search results have loaded, select the Xcode icon.

**Xcode**
Developer Tools
★★★★☆ 12 Ratings
Essentials
OPEN ▾

4.  Read the description and click the Install button. My screen shows OPEN because I already have Xcode installed.

# About the App We Are Going to Be Creating

There are an impressive number of dog lovers in the world, and you might be one of them. Some places, especially where I live, have rules about where dogs are or are not allowed, and also where dogs are allowed off the leash. We are going to focus on the OS X version of this application; motivated readers can also create iOS and web versions using CloudKit, synchronizing the data between them.

The primary features we are going to be focusing on are:

a.  Searching for dog-friendly parks (we will be focusing on North Vancouver, Canada)

b.  Finding specifically off-leash areas for your dog to run around free

c.  Finding specifically leash-required areas for dogs that are not comfortable off leash

d.  Adding new parks that other users of the app can see

e.  Approving/verifying user-created parks

f.  Uploading photos of your experiences at a specific park

g.  Viewing/creating reviews for dog parks

h.  Viewing/adding warnings; for example, bear in the area, aggressive dog, etc.

# Conclusion

This chapter provided an overview of what we will be creating over the course of this book, along with what is expected of you, the reader. In the next chapter we will dive into the planning of our app, get an overview of Sketch 3, and use Keynote for some basic animations of our app's user interface before moving onto coding.

■ ■ ■

# CHAPTER 2

# Prototyping Our App

Many times, developers jump into Xcode and start hacking away as soon as they have an idea. Although it is possible to create an application in this fashion, if you want to build a truly successful production app you should prototype first–or fake it until you make it. Apple has had a few presentations over the last few years at WWDC14 and WWDC15 that highlighted the importance of prototyping and user-testing apps.

In this chapter we are going to start with an overview of Sketch 3, then we will create the first version of our app. Finally, we will cover how to use KeyNote to add interactive animations to the mockup before starting to code.

## Introduction to Sketch 3

There has been a lot of hype about Sketch 3 over the last few years by designers and developers alike. I believe this has to do with its simplified user interface along with the way it sticks to its primary goal of creating user interfaces. A lot of graphics products try to be everything to everyone. When you first open Sketch you will really feel the difference as compared to a product such as Adobe PhotoShop. Figure 2-1 shows the main areas of the interface when you start a new project.

© Bruce Wade 2016
B. Wade, *OS X App Development with CloudKit and Swift*, DOI 10.1007/978-1-4842-1880-8_2

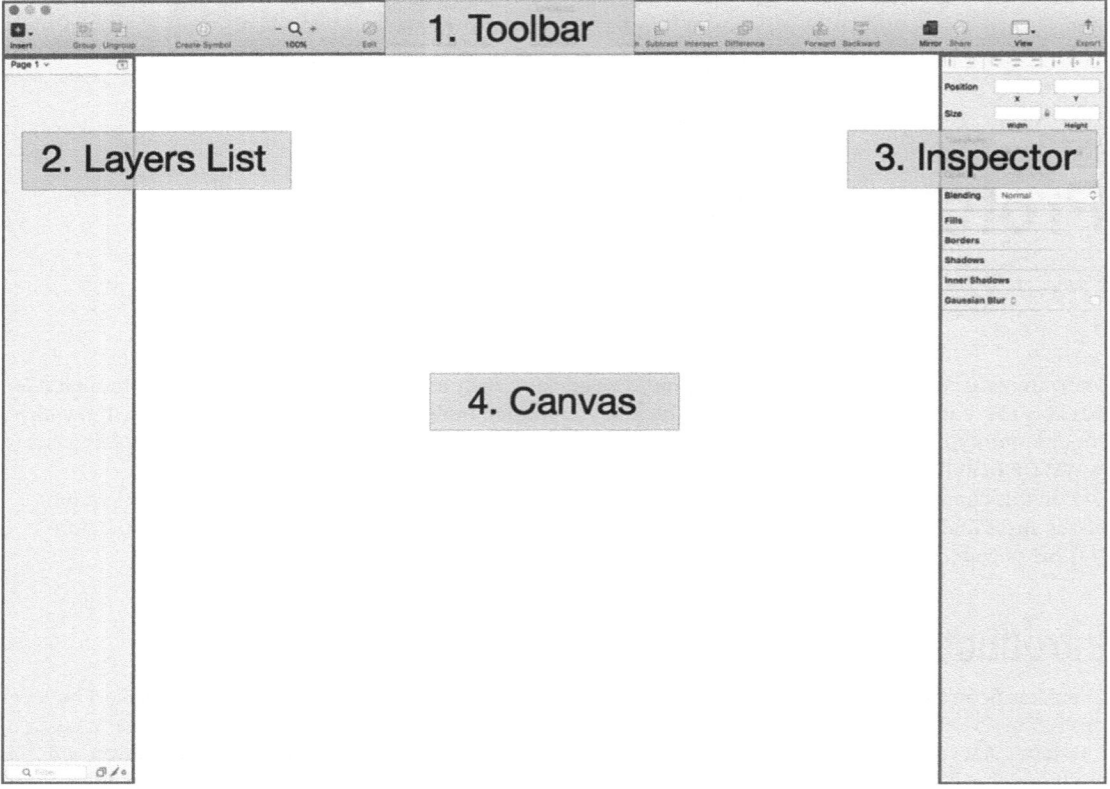

***Figure 2-1.*** *Blank Sketch 3 interface when starting a new project*

When starting your first project in Sketch, you might feel the interface is quite limited. Limited options and a simple interface aren't always a bad thing.

1. The toolbar is used for quick access to tools you will use often. You are not stuck with the default tools, however, as you can customize the toolbar to fit within your workflow.

    a. Right-click on the toolbar and select "Customize Toolbar." Figure 2-2 shows the popup menu with "Customize Toolbar" highlighted.

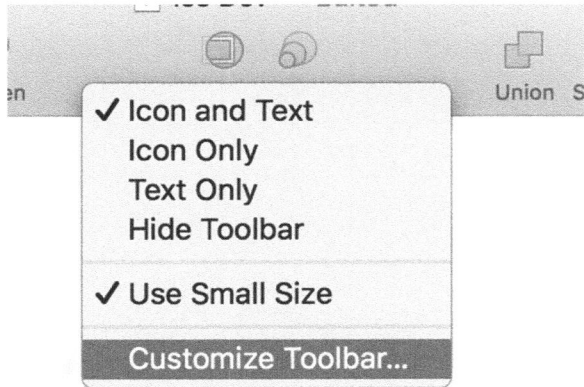

***Figure 2-2.*** *Menu when you right-click on the toolbar*

    b.    You will be taken to a view that allows you to drag and drop to add or remove different toolbar items to or from your main toolbar (Figure 2-3). You most likely will not use this feature until you understand what each tool does; however, it is a good feature to be aware of.

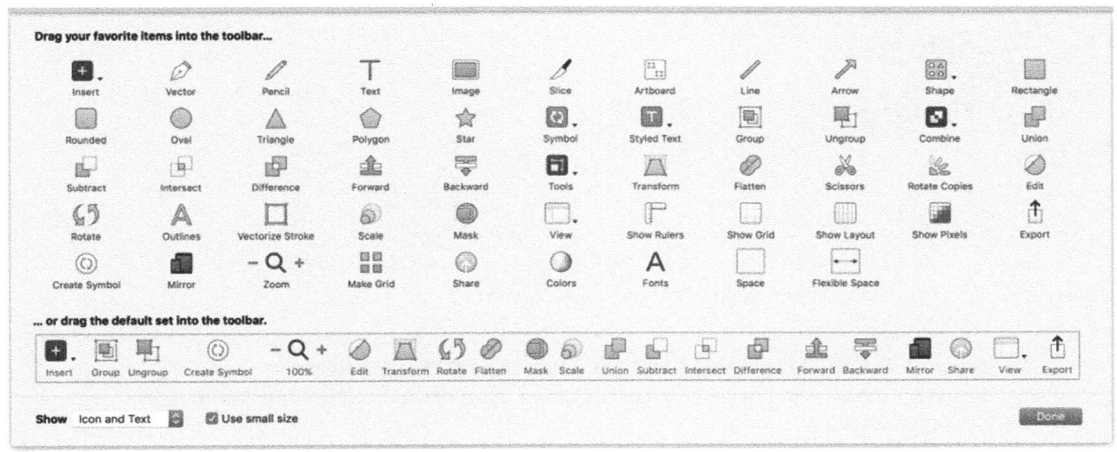

***Figure 2-3.*** *Options panel with all available options*

    2.    The Layers list area of the Sketch 3 interface allows you to organize your design into different layers and pages. Every object you add will be created on its own layer. You can then organize your page by grouping different layers together, as shown in Figure 2-4. The term *page* may be a little confusing unless you are familiar with web design. Basically it represents a unique view or feature of your app. It is used to allow you to better organize multiple designs into a single project file. You are able to create as many pages as you need (I don't think there is a limit; you would have to check the official documentation to know for sure), and you can have several layers per page.

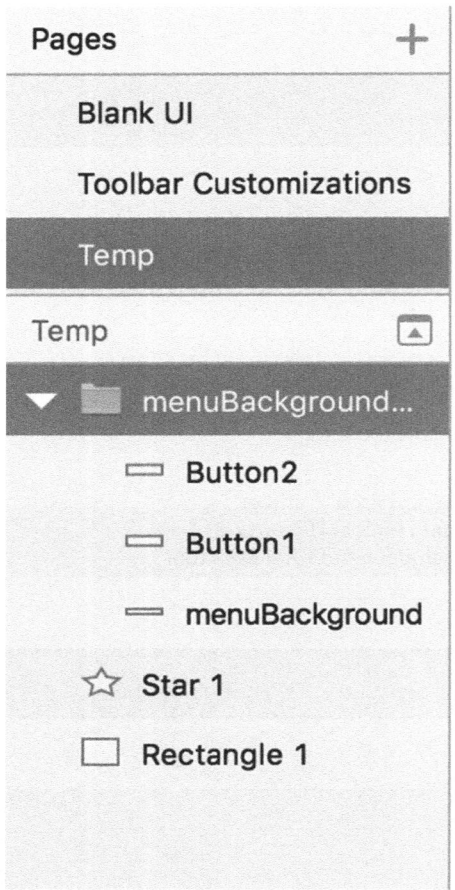

**Figure 2-4.** *Layer list panel showing multiple pages and layers*

3. Figure 2-4 shows a list of pages with the Temp page selected. You can see a list of layers for the selected page. You can click the + symbol on the Pages title bar to add another page.

4. The Inspector area is where you can customize the settings of any selected item that is on the canvas. The available settings dynamically change depending on what type of object you have selected. Figure 2-5 show the inspector options when creating an artboard.

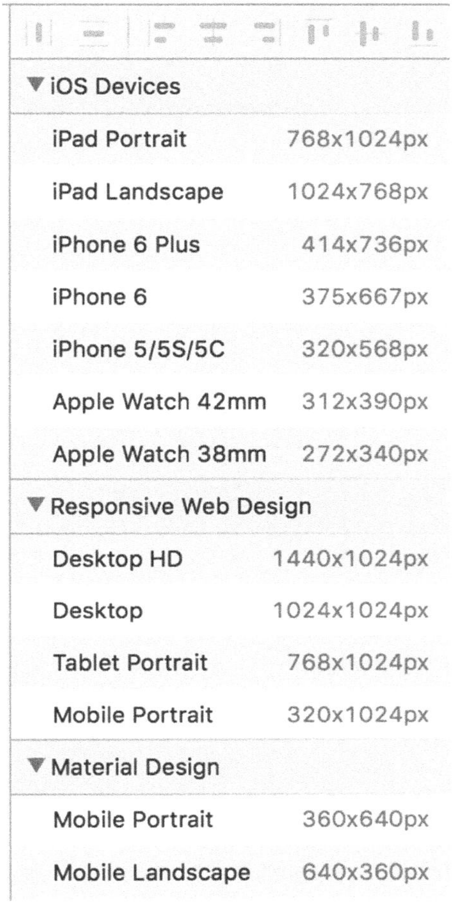

| iOS Devices | |
|---|---|
| iPad Portrait | 768x1024px |
| iPad Landscape | 1024x768px |
| iPhone 6 Plus | 414x736px |
| iPhone 6 | 375x667px |
| iPhone 5/5S/5C | 320x568px |
| Apple Watch 42mm | 312x390px |
| Apple Watch 38mm | 272x340px |
| **Responsive Web Design** | |
| Desktop HD | 1440x1024px |
| Desktop | 1024x1024px |
| Tablet Portrait | 768x1024px |
| Mobile Portrait | 320x1024px |
| **Material Design** | |
| Mobile Portrait | 360x640px |
| Mobile Landscape | 640x360px |

***Figure 2-5.*** *Inspector options for creating an artboard*

5. The canvas is where you will be spending all your time creating the prototype of your app. The canvas is unlimited in both height and width. However, Sketch has a really cool feature called Artboards that allows you to have smaller individual canvases. This helps you organize your scenes in a more organized fashion as well as limits how much screen space you are actually taking up.

# Our Prototype Objective

We are going to be creating an OS X app that is used to manage dog-park information; it will be used with an iOS app in the future. This book will focus on the OS X and CloudKit app. However, there is a tutorial on my website (warplydesigned.com) if you wish to learn how to create the iOS version.

Figure 2-6 is the mockup we will be creating using Sketch. As this is a mockup, the final project might not look exactly like this; however, it will be very close.

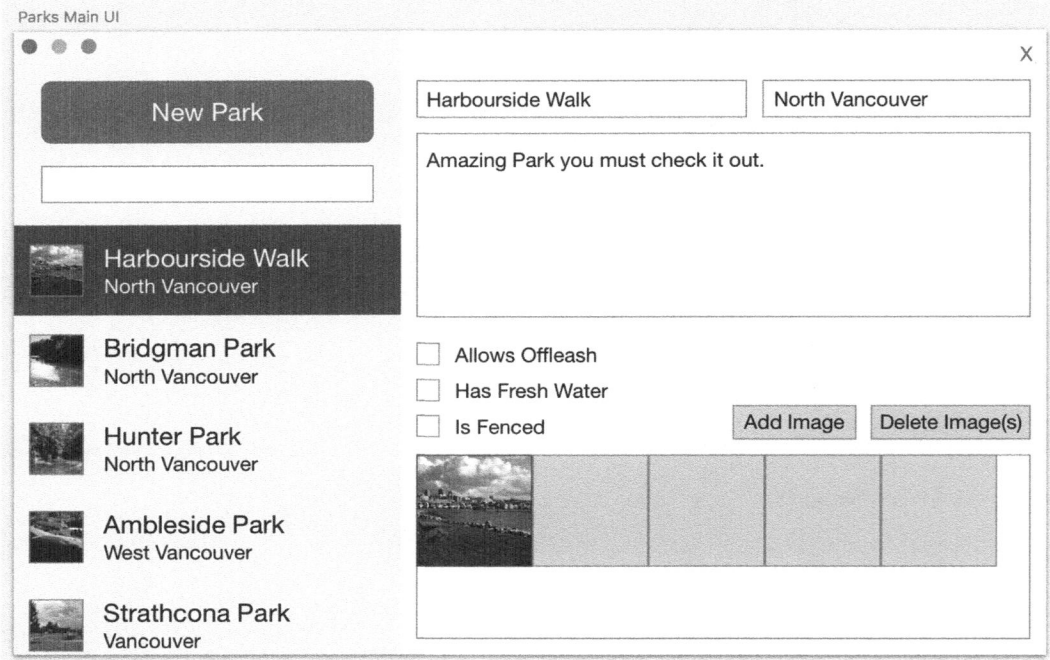

***Figure 2-6.*** *Dog parks app mockup*

# Building the Prototype with Sketch 3

It is time to build out our mockup using Sketch. We'll take a step-by-step approach in tackling the following main tasks:

1. Create the structure of the main window

2. Create the New Park button

3. Create the Search field

4. Create the park list

5. Create the last main content area

# Creating the Structure of the Main Window

In this section we are going to create the main window frame of our mockup, including the sidebar, main details area, and window control buttons.

1. Open up Sketch.

2. Press the A key. Your cursor will turn into a cross symbol, and the Inspector will provide you with a list of different screen resolutions for your new artboard. Instead of using one of the defaults, we are going to create one using custom dimensions.

3. With the cross symbol, click and drag out a rectangle. Don't worry about the exact size, as we will cover how to adjust it next.

4. Once you release your mouse, the Inspector will show options for the artboard's position and size. Adjust the size to a width of 800 and a height of 500. (It is important to remember you can create as many additional artboards on the canvas as you require.)

5. Next, press the R key for the rectangle tool. We are going to create the left sidebar. Starting at the top left-hand corner of the artboard, drag a rectangle that is 300 x 500 pixels. Don't worry about being exact, as you can use the Inspector to make things more exact.

6. With the new rectangle selected, uncheck the checkbox under the Borders heading in the Inspector panel. This is shown in Figure 2-7.

***Figure 2-7.*** *Border color disabled*

7.  Click on the Color box. In the Color dialog's Hex textbox, enter the value F5F7F7. See Figure 2-8.

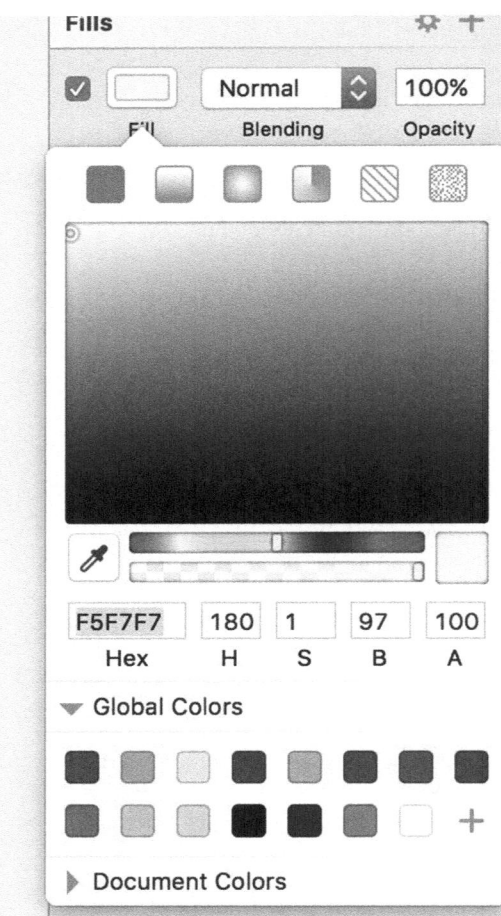

**Figure 2-8.** *Sidebar color being used*

8. In the Layers list, double-click Rectangle 1 to rename the layer to Left Sidebar.

9. While we are at it, double-click Artboard 1 to rename the page to Parks Main UI.

10. When done, your screen should look like the following (Figure 2-9); if not, recheck the steps.

***Figure 2-9.*** *Main window with sidebar and main content areas*

11. Next, let's create the close, minimize, and maximize buttons. Select Insert ➤ Shape ➤ Oval. (Also note that this is where you can get access to all the drawing tools available in Sketch 3). See Figure 2-10.

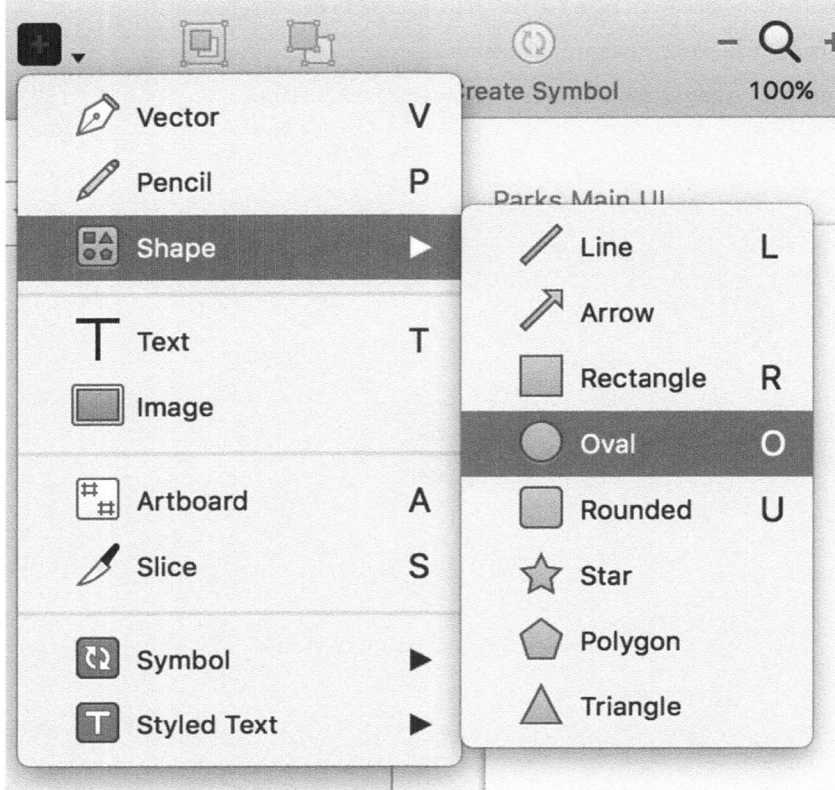

*Figure 2-10.* *Insert menu for shapes*

12. Draw an oval that is 12 pixels by 12 pixels. If you hold down the Shift key as you drag, you will create a perfect circle. This also works if you want to create a square from a rectangle. (Remember, you can adjust the size in the Inspector panel if needed.)

13. Now we need more copies of the circle you just created, so hold down the Option key and drag the circle to the left; release the mouse then the Option key. This creates a duplicate of the selected object. Do this one more time.

14. Next, let's position the circles in a horizontal line 8 points away from each other. Sketch provides a helpful tool to help you visualize this. First, select the circle you want to move by single clicking on the object. Next, hover your mouse over the object you want it to be 8 points away from. Finally pressing and holding down the option key will show you a red line with a number representing the distances the objects are from each other. Using the arrow keys on your keyboard, move the selected object to the left or right until the number shows 8 points. You can leave your mouse hovering over the target object as you move your selected object. Repeat the same process for the last circle.

15. Next, select all three circles by single-clicking on the first one, then holding down shift and clicking on the other two one by one. Next, with the circles selected, move your mouse over the left sidebar, then press and hold the Option key so you can see the distance guides. Next, using your arrow keys, move the circles to the left and top until they are 6 points from the top and 6 points from the left. You may have to use the magnifying glass to zoom in to see the distance correctly. If all went as expected your circles should look like Figure 2-11. If your colors are different don't worry, we will correct that next.

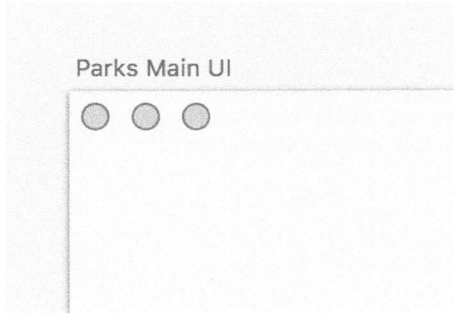

***Figure 2-11.*** *Control buttons at the top of our window's sidebar*

16. Let's move on to correcting the colors. Select the first circle on the left and click the fill color box in the Inspector panel. Set the hex value to F4554D and uncheck the border option.

17. Set the middle circle's fill color to F2B121 and uncheck the border option.

18. Finally, set the last circle's fill color to 0EBD35 and uncheck the border option. Your circles should now look like those in Figure 2-12.

***Figure 2-12.*** *Colored control buttons to match Apple's default OS X colors*

19. Next, let's clean up our layers a little. Select Oval 1 by clicking on it, then hold Shift and select Oval 1 Copy 2 to select all three circles (Figure 2-13).

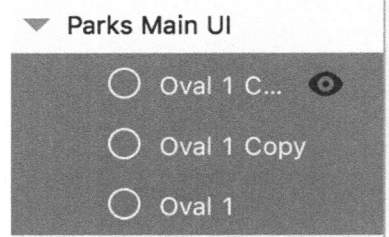

***Figure 2-13.*** *Three control buttons selected*

20. Press Command + G to group the circles together. Double-click the group and name it Window Controls. Optionally, you can rename each of the control circles. The green one is the Maximize button, orange is Minimize, and red is the Close button. See Figure 2-14.

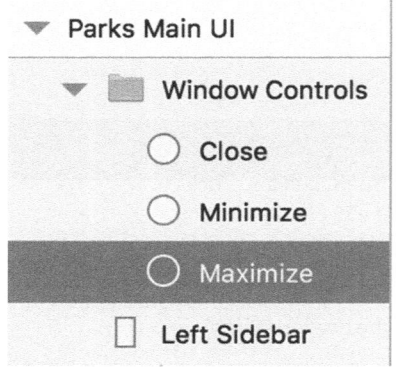

***Figure 2-14.*** *Control buttons in the Window Controls group, with each button renamed to match its function*

## Creating the New Park Button

Let's create the New Park button. To do so, follow these steps.

1. Press the R key and drag a rectangle so it appears on the right sidebar just below the control buttons. We will position this properly later. Make the button 258 x 50, with a position of 21 points from the left and 40 points from the top.

2. In the Inspector properties for the button, change the radius to 8 to give it rounded corners. (You could have also created a rounded rectangle using the U key.)

3. Uncheck the borders checkbox.

4. Set the fill color box hex to 4A90E2.

5. In the Layers panel, rename Rectangle 2 to Background.

6.   Press the T key and type in New Park over top of the button we just created. Make sure the New Park Text layer is placed above the layer you renamed in the previous step, or the text will not be visible.

7.   Give the text a size of 20 and set its color to white.

8.   Next, we are going to center the text using the alignment tools. First, select the text layer, then hold Shift and click on the button background. Next, in the Inspector properties click Align Horizontal, then click Align Vertical. (It is important to select these in the correct order to get this to work.)

9.   With both the text field and the background still selected, press Command + G to group them. Name the group New Park Button.

10.  Your project should look like the screenshot in Figure 2-15.

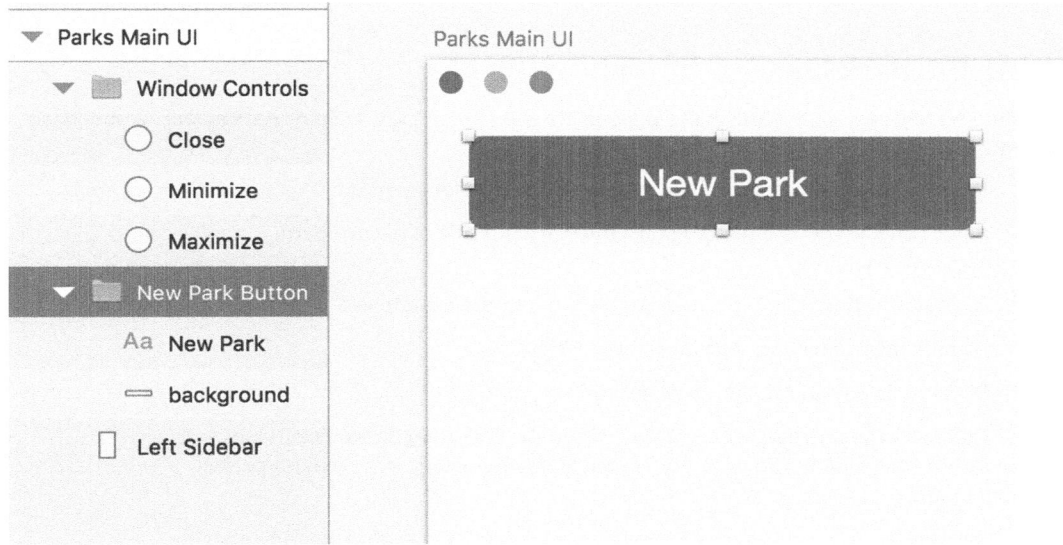

***Figure 2-15.*** *New Park button and the group for the button in the layers panel*

## Creating the Search Field

Next, we will create the Search field.

1.   Press the R key and drag out a rectangle under the New Park button.

2.   Make the rectangle 258 x 30.

3.   Position the rectangle 21 points from the left and 18 points from the New Park button. (Hover your mouse over the New Park button, then press and hold the Option key to see the spacing guidelines. Then use your keyboard arrow keys to put the rectangle into place.)

4.   Set the rectangle's fill color to white and its border color to a gray, 979797.

5.   Rename the Rectangle 3 layer to Search Box. See Figure 2-16.

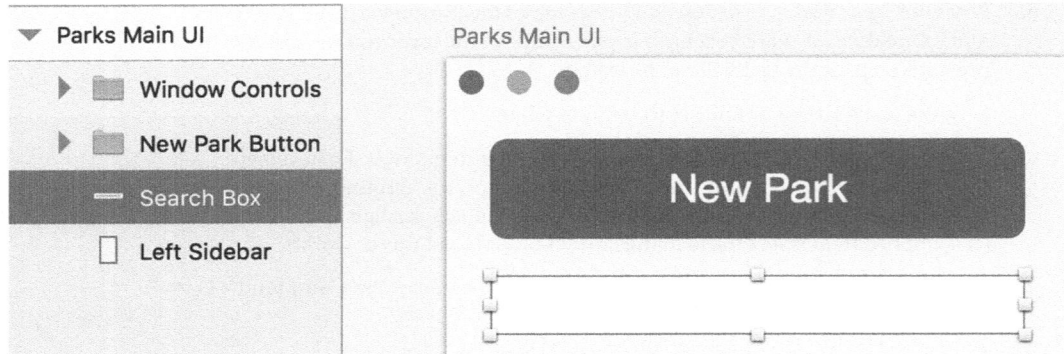

**Figure 2-16.** *Search box under the New Park button*

## Creating the Park List

In this section we will create park lists in the sidebar. We will also create a selected park as well as show non-selected parks.

1. Press the R key and drag out a rectangle; this will be for a park row.

2. Make sure the row is directly against the left-hand side of the artboard, with a size of 300 x 72.

3. Its position should be X = 0, and 18 points below the Search box.

4. Disable the border and set a fill color to 0066DC.

5. Rename the layer Park Item Background.

6. Create another rectangle size 42 x 42 within the Park Item Background. This will be our Image View. (You can hold down Shift while dragging to make a perfect square.)

7. Position the new Image View 12 points from the left, 15 points from the top of the Park Item Background, and 15 points from the bottom. To see the distance, hover your mouse over the Park Item Background, and with the Image View selected hold down the Option key.

8. Set the background color to F5F7F7 and the border color to 979797.

9. Next, we will add the labels. Press the T key and type Harbourside Walk beside the Image View.

10. Make sure the new text field is above the Park Item Background in the Layers list.

11.  Set the text color to white and size to 20 points.

12.  Align the text 14 points from the top of the Park Item Background and 16 points from the Image View.

13.  Press the T key again and type North Vancouver under the previous text field; this is the park's location.

14.  Set the size to 16 points, and position it 16 points from the Image View and 14 points from the bottom of the Park Item Background.

15.  Now, in the Layer list select both text fields, the Image View, and the Park Item Background, then press Command + G to group them. Name the group Dog Park (Figure 2-17).

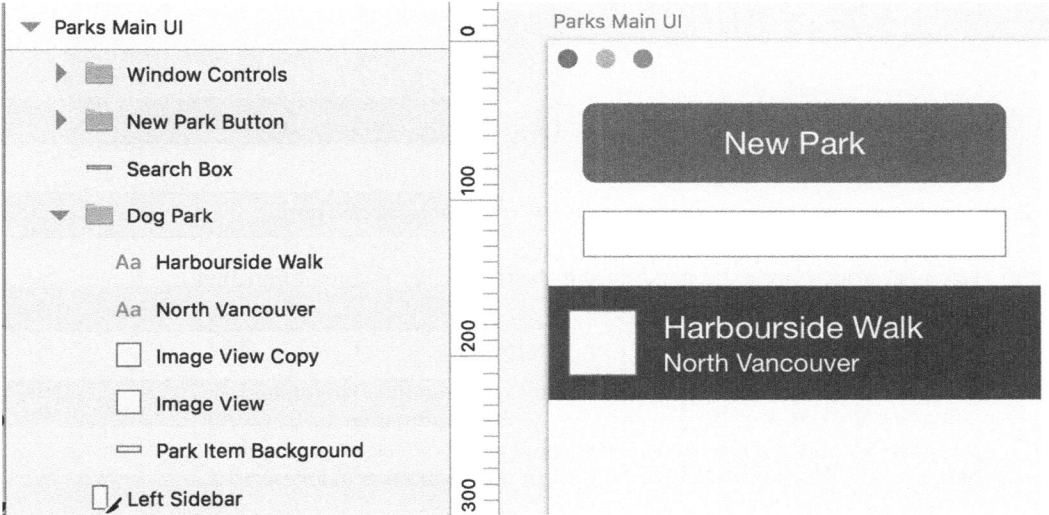

***Figure 2-17.*** *Example of how a selected park will look*

16.  Select the Dog Park group and press Command + D to make a duplicate copy.

17.  With the Dog Park Copy group selected, use your down arrow key to move the copy on the artboard to be below the Dog Park group you previously created. See Figure 2-18.

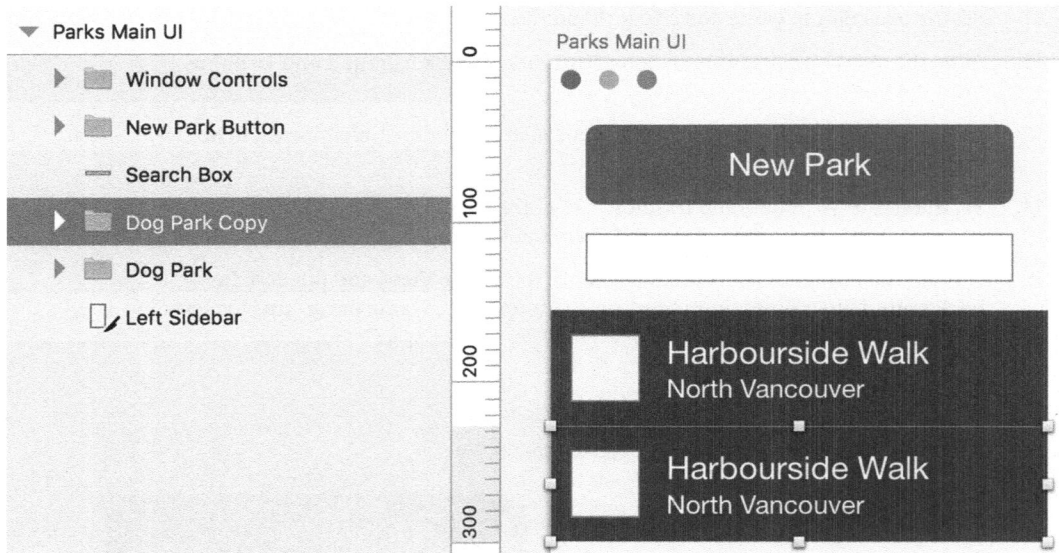

***Figure 2-18.*** *Duplicate of selected park that we will use to create non-selected park*

18.  Open the group copy you just moved and change the fill color of the Park Item Background to F5F7F7.

19.  Select both text views and change their color to black.

20.  Now select the Dog Park Copy group and press Command + D to duplicate it. Using your keyboard, move the new group on the artboard to be below the previous Dog Park group you just placed. Repeat this process two more times to have a total of four copies. Your artboard should look like that in Figure 2-19.

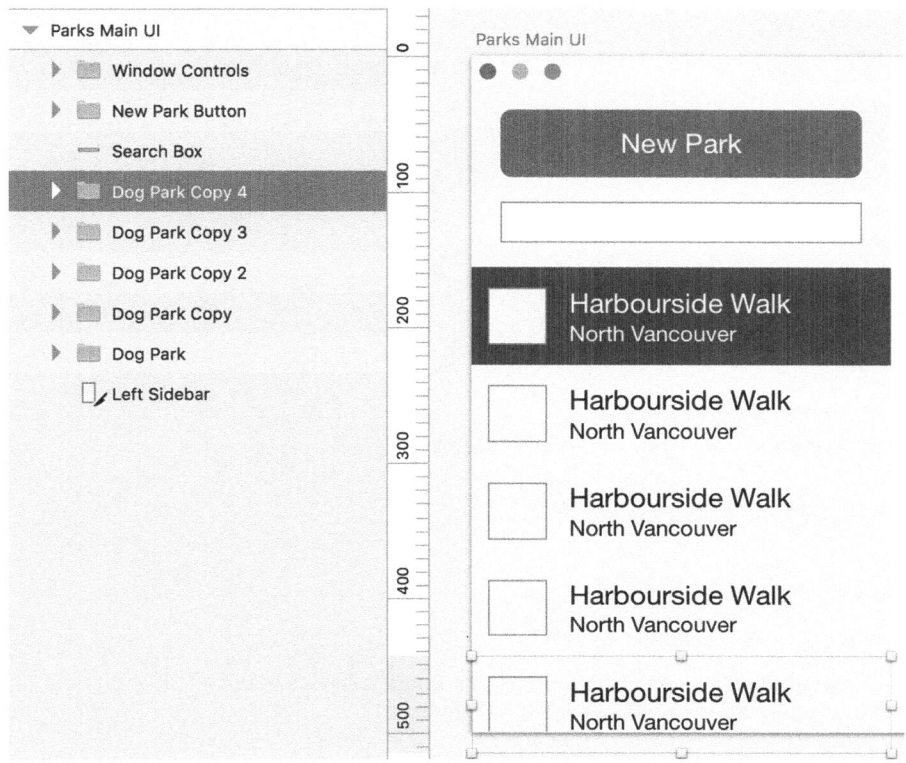

***Figure 2-19.*** *Park list with both a selected park and non-selected parks*

21. Finally, select all the Dog Park copies, as well as the original Dog Park group, and group them, naming the group Park List. See Figure 2-20.

***Figure 2-20.*** *All of the parks grouped into a parent Park List group*

This completes our sidebar.

## Creating a New Group

I like to keep things as neat as possible, cleaning up as I go:

1. Select the entire layers group along with the Search box and left sidebar and group them into a new group called Left Sidebar (Figure 2-21).

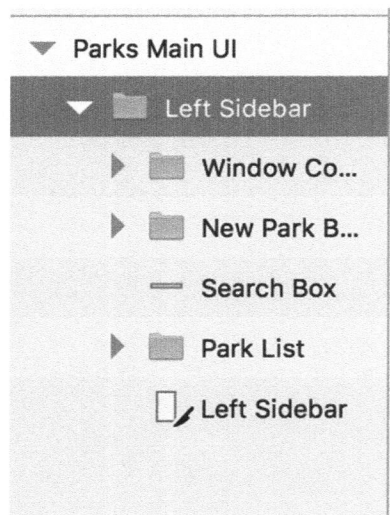

***Figure 2-21.*** *Master group of left sidebar*

2. Right-click the Left Sidebar group and choose "Lock Layer." This will prevent us from accidentally moving any item on the sidebar. See Figure 2-22.

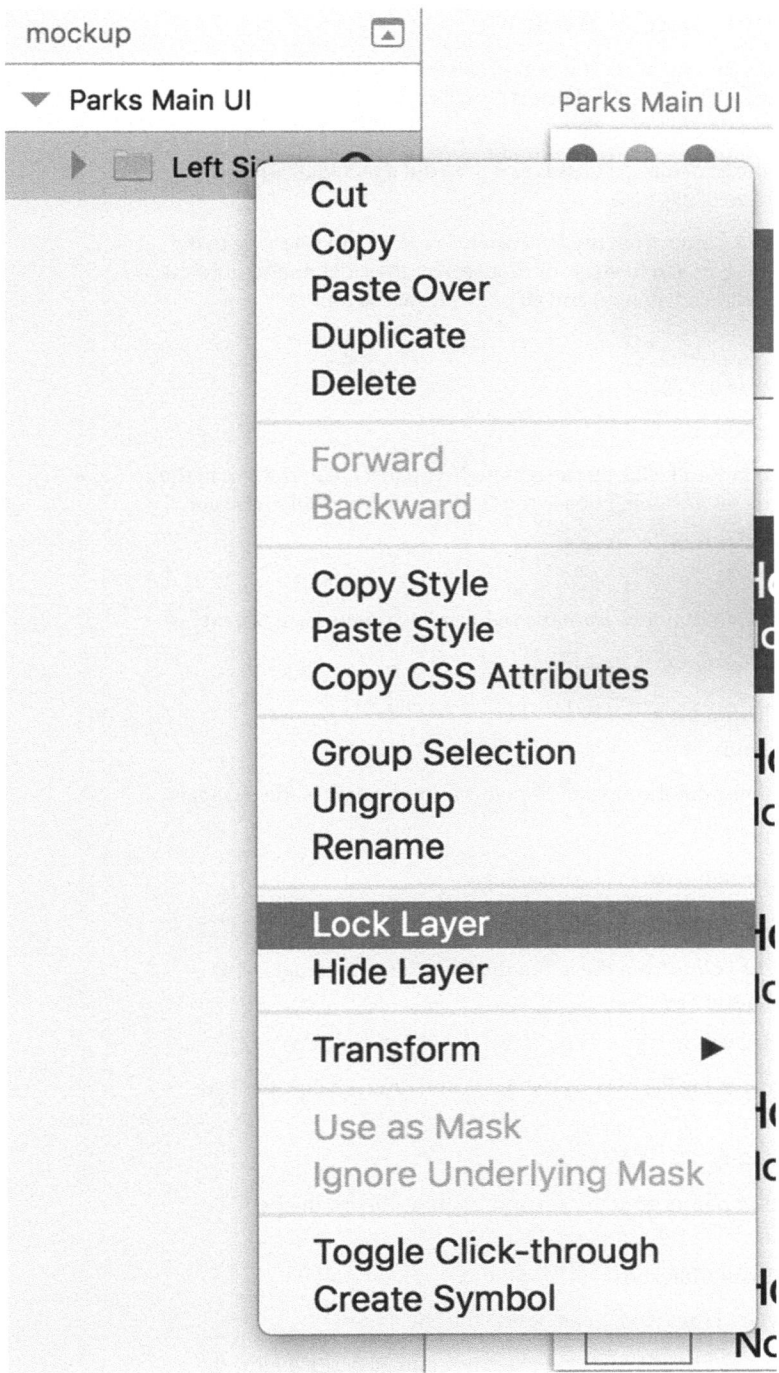

*Figure 2-22.* *View of menu when you right-click on a group so you can lock the layer (group and all layers within it)*

# Creating Another Main Content Area

Now it's time to create the last main content area. This will consist of creating multiple textboxes (similar to the Search box we have already created), some checkboxes (small rectangles), and finally a box filled with other boxes that will resemble our collection of images.

1. Create a text field for the park name. Press R and drag out a rectangle in the main content area with the size of 256 x 30.

2. Position the rectangle 12 points from the left (when I say *left* I am referring to the right edge of the left sidebar; just hover your mouse over the sidebar and hold the Option key to see the correct distance) and 40 points from the top.

3. Set the fill color to white.

4. Set the border fill color to 979797.

5. Rename the layer Park Name.

6. Hold down the Option key and click on the rectangle you just created. Drag to the right and release the rectangle, then release the Option key. This will duplicate the Park Name rectangle.

7. Set the size to 208 x 30.

8. Position the new rectangle 12 points from the right and 40 points from the top.

9. Rename the layer Park Location.

10. Press the T key, and in the top right-hand corner type a capital X.

11. Set the text size to 16 points.

12. Align the X to be 10 points from the top and 10 points from the right of the rectangle.

13. Set its color to red.

14. Make another duplicate of the Park Name rectangle.

15. Set its size to 446 x 148 points.

16. Set the position to be 12 points from the left of the Park Name rectangle, and from the right edge of the artboard.

17. Rename the layer Park Overview.

18. Make another duplicate of the Park Name rectangle and drag it below the Park Overview rectangle.

19. Set its size to 18 x 18 points.

20. Position the rectangle 12 points from the left and 20 points below the Park Overview rectangle.

21. Rename the layer Offleash Checkbox.

22. Press the T key and type Allows Offleash beside the checkbox.

23. Align this rectangle to be 12 points from the checkbox and 20 points below the Park Overview rectangle.

24. Set the color to black (hex code: 000000).

25. Select both the checkbox and the text layer you just created and create a group (Command + G). Name the group Option Offleash.

26. With the group selected in the Layers list, press Command + D to duplicate.

27. Using your down arrow key, move the new group 10 points below the Allows Offleash checkbox.

28. Make another duplicate and move it 10 points below the checkbox group you just created.

29. Now rename the group for the middle option to Option Fresh Water.

30. Open the Fresh Water option and select the text layer. Then double-click on the text on the artboard and change it to Has Fresh Water.

31. Rename the bottom option group Option Fenced.

32. Open the Fenced option group and select the text layer. Then double-click on the text in the artboard and change it to Is Fenced. (You can also just keep clicking on the text until you are able to select it.)

33. Next, let's set up the Image Collection View. Create a rectangle that is 476 x 148 points and position it 12 points from the left, right, and bottom.

34. Set the fill color to white (hex code FFFFFF).

35. Rename the layer Collect View.

36. Create a rectangle that is 90 x 90 points and position it inside the Collection View against the top and left borders.

37. Set the fill color to D8D8D8.

38. Rename the rectangle Collection Image View.

39. Make four more copies of the Collection Image View and position them against the edge of the box on the left. See Figure 2-23.

***Figure 2-23.*** *Collection of images*

40. Change the border color of the first Image View to 0066DC.

41. In the Layers list, select the Collection View and all the Collection Image Views and group them. Name the new group Park Images Collection.

42. Next, we need two final buttons–one for adding images, the other for deleting them.

43. Create a rectangle that is 124 x 28 points and is positioned 12 points from the right and 12 points above the Collection View rectangle.

44. Use the text tool to type the text Delete Image(s) and center it inside the just-created rectangle.

45. Group the text and rectangle, naming the group Image Delete Button.

46. Next, make a duplicate of the Image Delete Button group and name it Add Image Button.

47. Move the Add Image Button group to be 12 points from the left side of the Delete Image(s) button and 12 points above the Collection View.

48. Replace the text on the Delete Image button with Add Image. Make sure to realign it.

49. Select all the layers except the Left Sidebar group and create a new group named Park Details.

50. Now our mockup is complete, and should look like that in Figure 2-24.

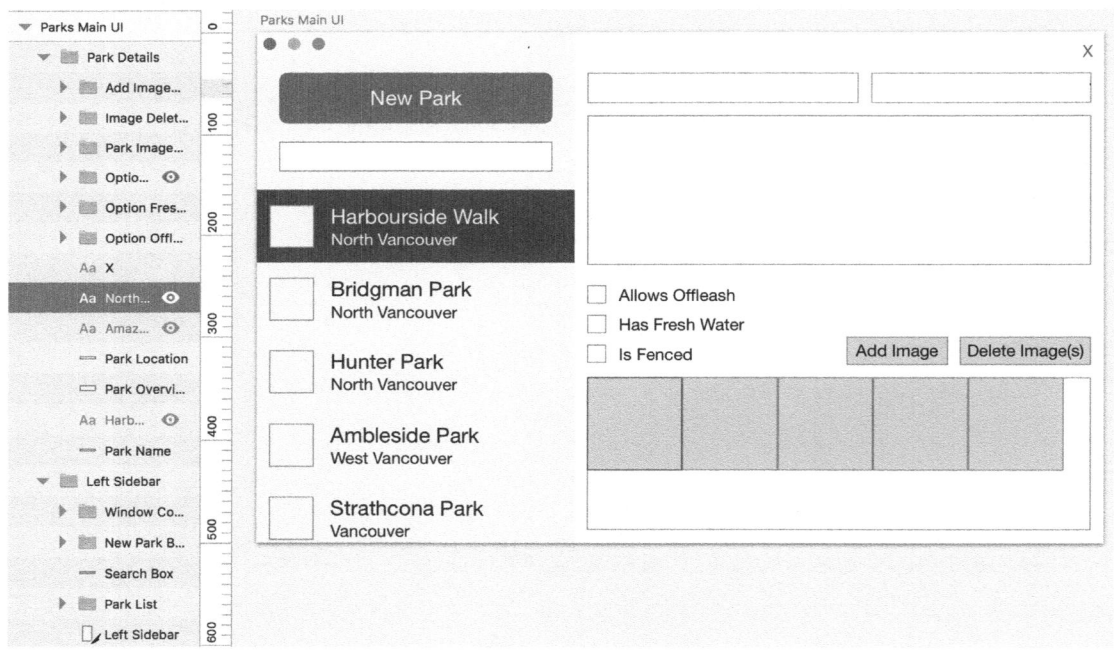

*Figure 2-24.* *Final mockup*

# Making the Prototype More Real

Before moving on to KeyNote, we need to make some changes to our prototype and create a few more artboards. Luckily, all the hard work is already done, so these changes are minor. All you need to do is follow these steps:

1. Update the park names and locations so they are all different. See Figure 2-25.

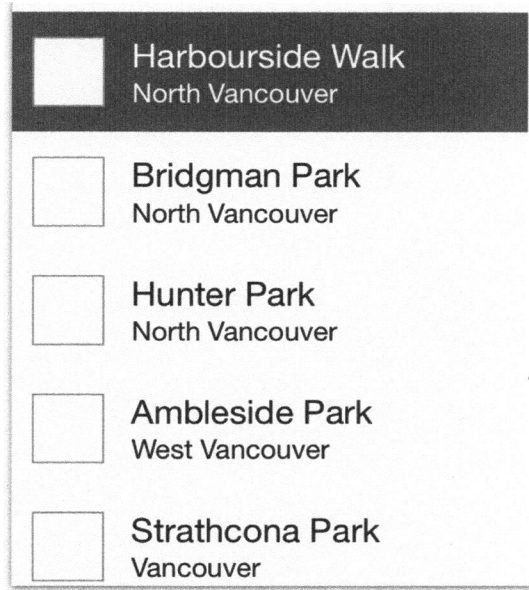

*Figure 2-25.* *Park list with updated park names and locations*

2. Let's add an example image for each of the parks in the list. First, click the Image View for Harbourside Walk. Next, click the fill color box and click on the pattern fill button, which is the fifth from the left. Click the Browse button to find the picture you want. Finally, set the image to fill (in the drop-down menu below the Browse button). See Figure 2-26.

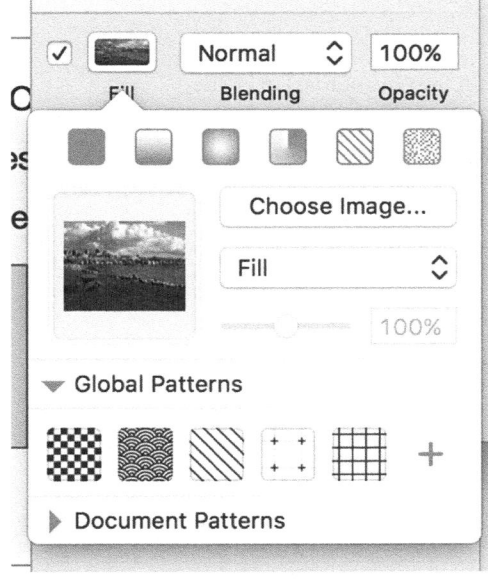

*Figure 2-26.* *Fill pattern option that enables us to select an image*

3. Repeat the process for the other parks in the list. When you are done, your new list will look something like that in Figure 2-27.

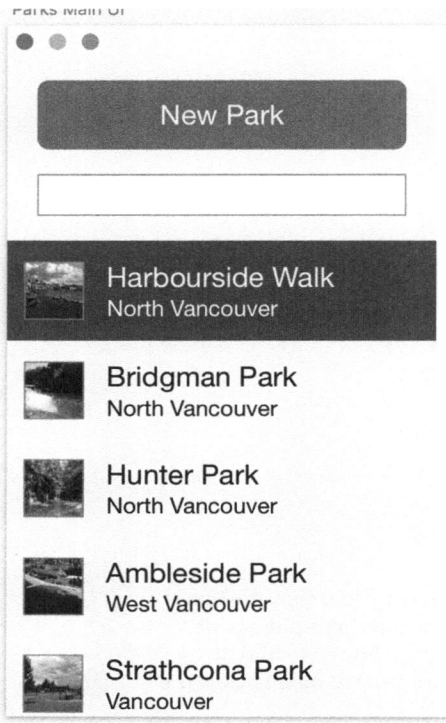

*Figure 2-27.* *Park list with updated park images*

4. Update the first Collection Image View (the one with the blue border) to be the same image as you used for the Harbourside Walk Image View.

5. In the Park Details panel, set the Park Name text field to `Harbourside Walk`.

6. Add `North Vancouver` to the Park Location text field.

7. Add the text `Amazing Park you must check it out.` inside the Park Overview section.

8. Your mockup should look like Figure 2-28.

**Figure 2-28.** *Collection View with an assigned image*

# Reviewing the Features We Want to Display Using KeyNote

We'll start by showing what searching for a park looks like. Then we'll show what adding a new park looks like.

## Searching for a Park

Let's make a duplicate of the finished artboard. Select the artboard (click on the name Parks Main UI). Then press Command + D. This will create an exact copy of the artboard. Name the new artboard Searching by double-clicking on the current title, Parks Main UI Copy. Then follow these steps:

1. Hover over each of the park list's items and then click the eye that shows up to hide that item.

2. Do the same process and hide the text for the name, location, and overview from the details panel.

3. Finally, hide all the Collection Image Views. When you are done, your Searching artboard should look like the following (Figure 2-29).

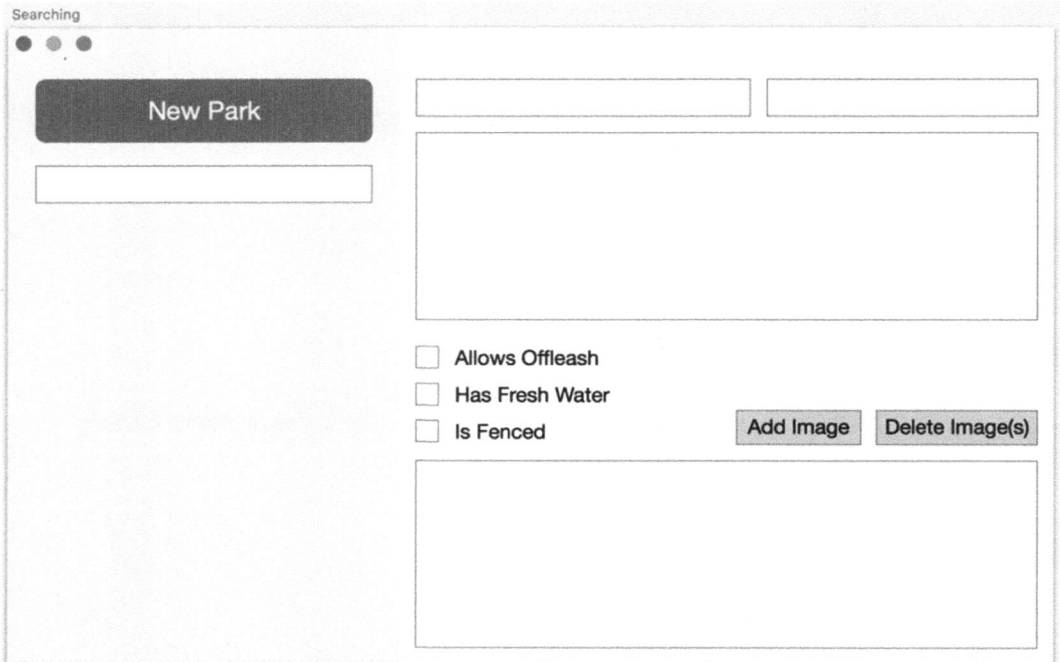

*Figure 2-29.* *Initial empty app screen*

4. Duplicate the Searching artboard and name it Search Results. Zoom out of your canvas a little bit by clicking the minus sign by the magnifying glass. Then drag the Search Results artboard to be below the Searching artboard.

5. Next, go through the search results layers and turn on the first Collection View Image that contains the image you just added. Turn back on the overview, location, name, and delete button (it looks like a red X).

6. Of all the park lists, turn on only Harbourside Walk.

7. Your two finished searching artboards should look like the following (Figure 2-30).

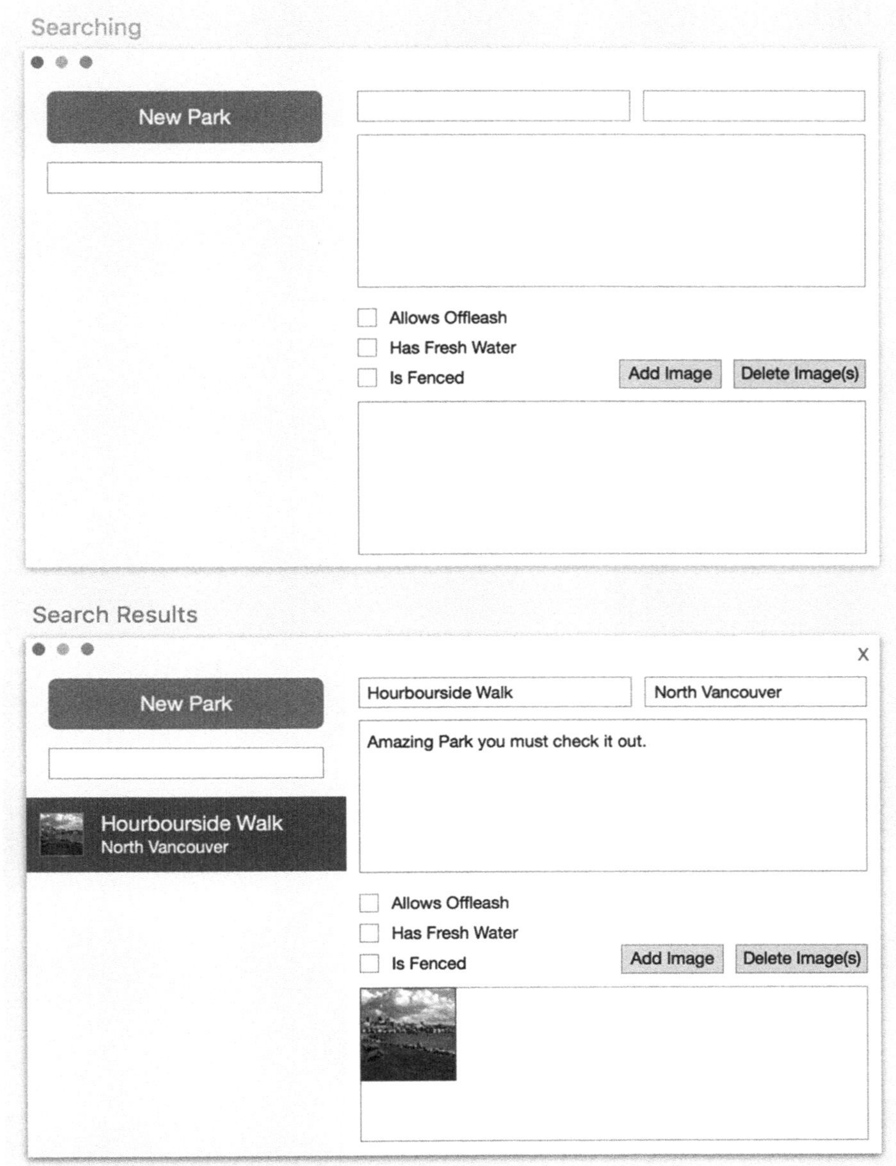

Searching

Search Results

*Figure 2-30.* *Searching and Search Results screens*

## Adding a New Park

1. Duplicate the artboard you used for Searching. Set its name to be New Park.

2. Set the first park list item to be visible.

3. Hide the Park Name and Park Location text fields.

4. Set the Image View to be a color background instead of an image (see Figure 2-31).

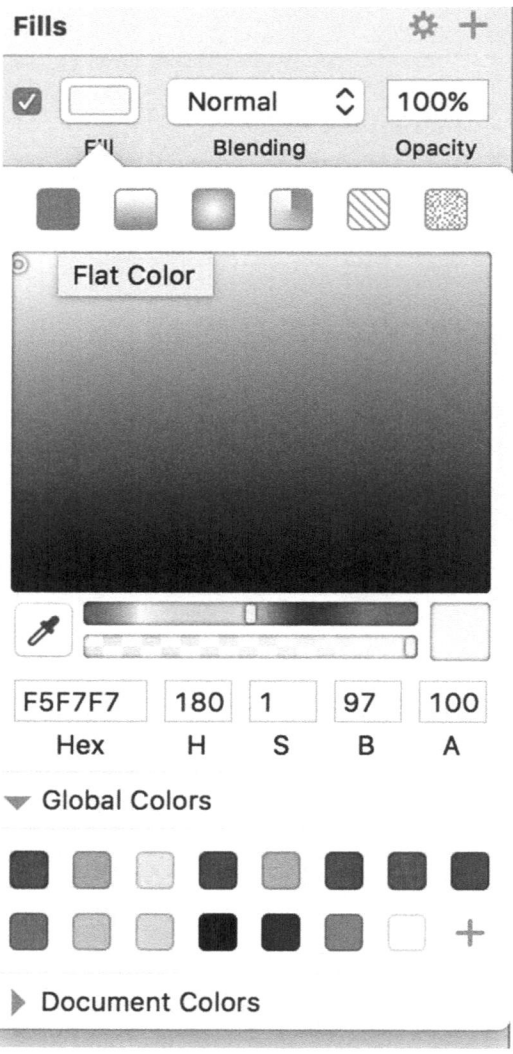

**Figure 2-31.** *Fill color selector*

5. Duplicate the artboard for New Park.

6. Insert the image `FileImageSelection` from the included files. Center it over the center of the artboard you just created.

7. Make another duplicate of the New Image artboard and name it Show Image. Enable the following:

   a. In the Parks List item, show the Park Name and Park Location and set the Image View background to be the image provided–harbourside_park_ourbc.png.

   b. In the image detail panel show Park Name, Park Location, Park Overview fields.

   c. Turn on the first Collection View Image item. Set its image background to be the same image as in the Park List Image View.

8. When you are finished, the artboard for Show Image should look like the bottom panel of Figure 2-32.

**Figure 2-32.** *The artboards we will be using in KeyNote*

## Exporting Artboards to Use Inside KeyNote

Exporting artboards is extremely easy in Sketch 3. You can export a complete artboard, groups, or individual layers. If there are any layers in a group that you would like to exclude from your export, simply toggle the eye that shows up when you mouse over a layer.

1. First, select the artboard you want to export from the Layers list by clicking on the artboard's name.

2. Next, at the bottom of the Inspector, click "Make exportable."

3. Select the checkbox for background color.

4. Finally, click "Export [Name of Artboard]."

5. Follow this process to export the following artboards: Search Results, Show Image, Image Selection, New Park, Searching, and Before Searching.

## Using KeyNote to Make a Realistic Demo

Let's look at a quick example of what can be done with KeyNote. If you spend enough time with KeyNote you could improve your prototype with animations (not covered here) to make it fairly realistic. This isn't an in-depth guide to KeyNote, however, as Apple provides good documentation for that.

1. Open KeyNote and select a template with a white background.

2. On the right-hand side in the Slide Layout click Edit Master Slide.

3. Take a screenshot of your computer's desktop.

4. Back in KeyNote, set the background to the screenshot image you just took, and choose "Scale to fill."

5. Click the Done button at the bottom of KeyNote in the blue bar.

6. Select Insert ➤ Choose to find the New Park artboard. This will place the artboard in the center of the slide.

7. Select the slide in the slide list and press Command + D to duplicate it.

8. Use the text tool to type an H in the Park Name field. In the Options panel select the Text tab, then align the text to the left.

9. Now select the H you just created, hold down the Option key, and drag the H (to duplicate it) to where the park name would be in the Park List (Figure 2-33).

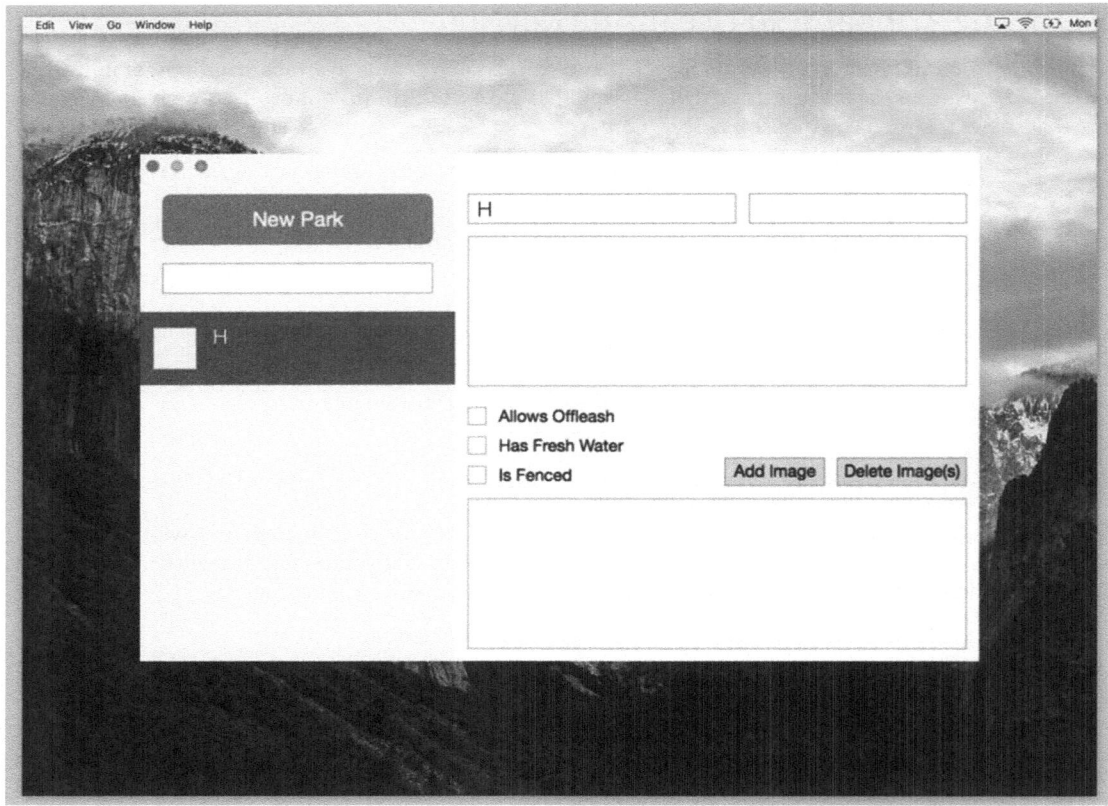

***Figure 2-33.*** *Shows how typing a letter should update both the detail and the park list for the selected park*

10. Select the slide you just created and press Command + D to duplicate it.

11. Update both text fields to include the letter a.

12. You can repeat the same process for each letter or fast track it. I will take the fast-track approach in this guide.

13. Duplicate the last slide and add rbourside to both text fields.

14. Duplicate the last slide and add Walk to both text fields.

15. Duplicate the last slide and use the text tool to type No in the detail screen's Park Location field. Duplicate that text and move it to the place in the Park List where the location should go.

16. Duplicate the last slide and add rth in both spots.

17. Duplicate the last slide and add Vancouver in both location text fields.

18. Duplicate the last slide and type Amazing you must check it out. inside the Park Details field.

19. Create a new slide by pressing the + button and use the master slide with your desktop background.

20. Insert the Image Selector artboard.

21. Repeat step 19.

22. Insert the Show Image artboard, which will show what the new park entry looks like after selecting an image and closing the file-selector dialog.

23. Repeat step 19.

24. Insert the Before Searching artboard.

25. Repeat step 19.

26. Insert the Searching artboard.

27. Use the text feature to type H in the search box.

28. Duplicate the last slide.

29. Add ar to the search field.

30. Repeat step 19.

31. Insert the Search Results artboard.

32. Select the very first slide, then click the Play button; click the arrows to cycle through all the slides.

33. That's it! We are done with our first prototype. Feel free to continue playing around with your slides to make the flow look more realistic.

# Conclusion

This was definitely a long chapter, but we have covered many things. This includes creating a simple prototype application using Sketch, as well as a quick overview of using Keynote to see how the app will function in the real world. Resist the urge to skip prototypes and jump directly into coding. The more prototypes you do the better your applications will become. If you haven't watched Apple's keynotes on prototypes, you should take a break from reading now and spend some time watching them:

1. Prototyping: Fake It Till You Make It
   https://developer.apple.com/videos/play/wwdc2014-223/

2. Designing for the Future Hardware
   https://developer.apple.com/videos/play/wwdc2015-801/

3. Designing with Animation
   https://developer.apple.com/videos/play/wwdc2015-803/

■ ■ ■

# CHAPTER 3

# Defining Our Data

Now that we have our app's rough prototype, we can figure out what data we need to store in our app. In this chapter we will look at the different features of our mockup and break them down into data categories and types. Finally, we will create the first pass of our app so that in the next chapter we can shift our focus to CloudKit.

The mockup we created is intentionally simple and lacks certain features so that we can focus on the basic flow of going from idea to complete app.

## Taking a Closer Look at Our Mockup

Figure 3-1 shows our completed mockup.

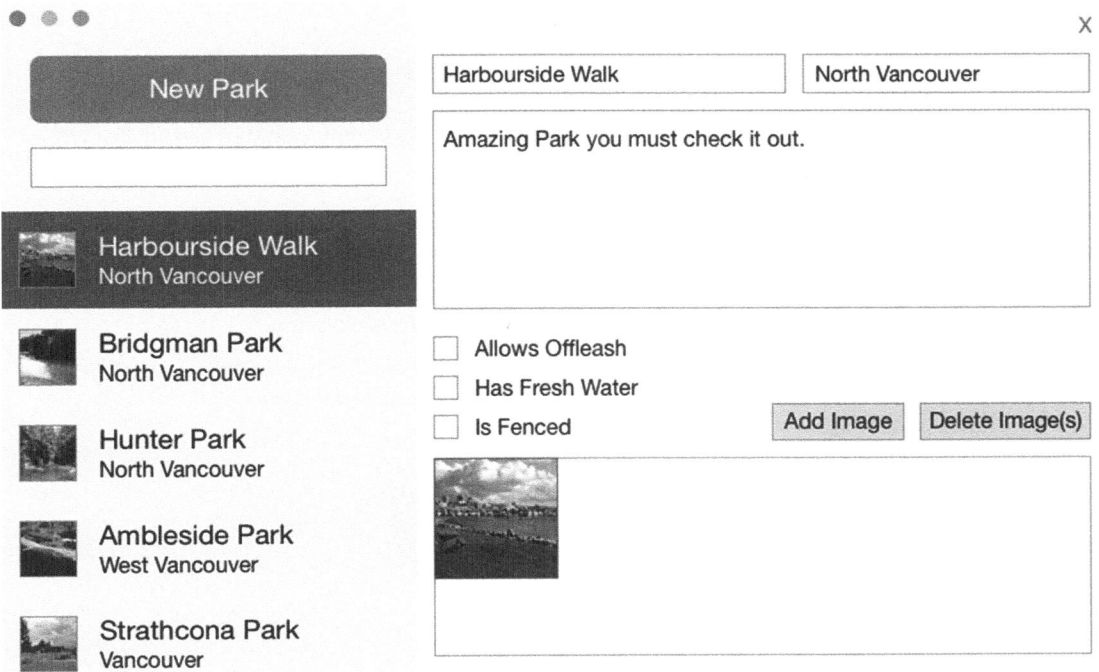

***Figure 3-1.*** *Mockup from where we left off in the last chapter*

© Bruce Wade 2016
B. Wade, *OS X App Development with CloudKit and Swift*, DOI 10.1007/978-1-4842-1880-8_3

In looking at the mockup, it seems the information we need to keep track of includes the following:

- Dog park details (Name, Location, Overview, Allows Offleash, Has Fresh Water, Is Fenced)

- List of images

- List of parks

From this we can determine we need at least two objects to get started–one object to hold an individual park, and one to hold the park's images. For the list of parks we can just use the built-in list data structure.

# Dog Park Data Types

Here are the park data types:

- Name – String type

- Location – Here we are also going to use a String; however, for a challenge you could change this to use the NSLocation type, which is also supported by CloudKit.

- Overview – String type

- Allows Offleash – Boolean

- Has Fresh Water – Boolean

- Is Fenced – Boolean

- Images – List of Park Images

# Creating Our Project in Xcode

We are going to use storyboards and Cocoa Bindings so as to write the minimal amount of code that will enable us to achieve our goals:

1. Open Xcode and create a new Xcode project.

2. Select "Cocoa Application," which can be found in the OS X Application section. Click Next.

3. Enter DogParks (or a name of your choice) for the Product Name.

4. Enter your organization name in the Organization name field, or if you don't have one enter your own name. (If you have set this up in the past it will be prepopulated for you.)

5. Make sure to select Swift as the programming language.

6. Check the box next to Storyboards, as we will be using them for our app.

7. Deselect all other checkboxes.

8. Click Next and pick the location where you want to save your app.

9. You can optionally select "Create Git Repository"; however, we will not be covering version control in this book.

# Update the Main.storyboard

Now we have to make some changes to the storyboard to get the design we have in our mockup. The default storyboard has a single view controller connected to the window controller. Select the view controller and delete it. Now the window controller says "No Content View Controller."

In the Objects Library either scroll through the objects to find the vertical split view controller or type it in the search filter at the bottom of the Objects Library. Drag the vertical split view controller to the position where the view controller you just deleted was. While you are at it, reorganize the two view controllers that are part of the vertical split view controller to be directly under it instead of to the right.

Next, we need to connect the window controller to the new vertical split view controller. Click on the window controller icon, then press Control and click and drag the icon to the vertical split view controller, and in the popup dialog select "Window Content."

If you were to run the application now, something strange would happen. You might not see a window as you would expect. However, if you were to look closer you'd see the window is there, but is only a single gray line. This is because the vertical split view controller is dependent on autolayout. We will add the required constraints as we go.

# Creating the Left Sidebar

Let's start by taking a closer look at the sidebar from our mockup (Figure 3-2) to determine what objects Xcode provides that we can use to achieve our goals.

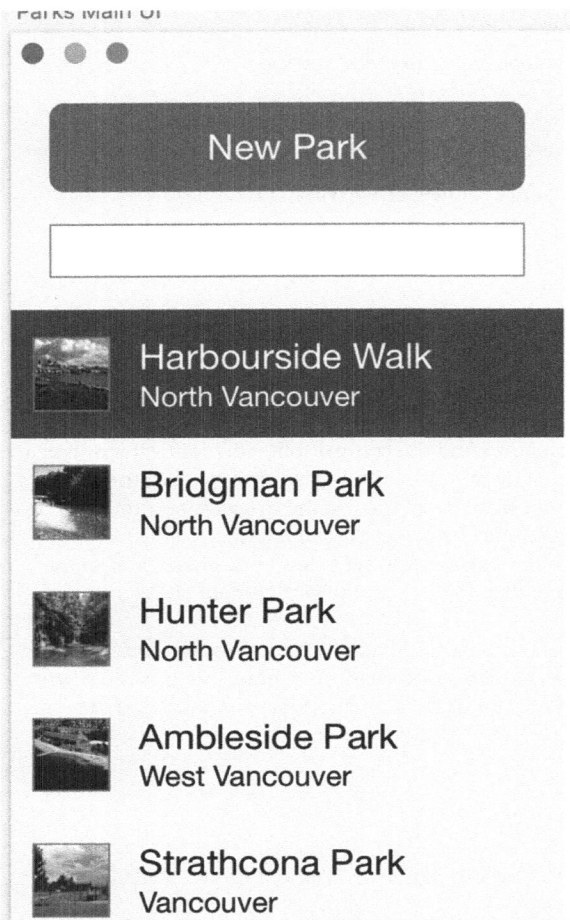

**Figure 3-2.** *Sidebar of the mockup*

We can use a button image for the New Park button, a Search field, a Table View that contains an Image View, and two labels. We don't have to worry about the close/minimize/maximize buttons, as Xcode handles this for us automatically.

Before we start dragging objects onto our view, we need to adjust the size of the sidebar to what we had in our mockup. To do this, select the view in the outline for the left-most view controller of the vertical split view controller (Figure 3-3).

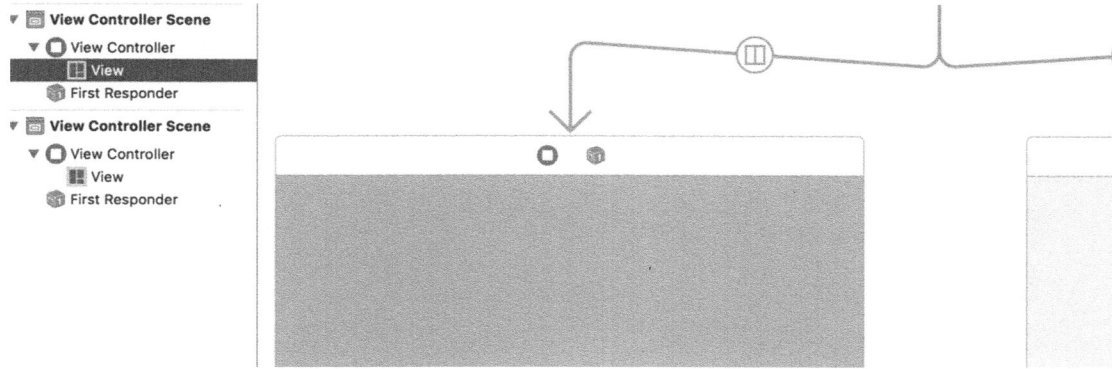

**Figure 3-3.** *Selecting the view of the view controller*

Next, in the Size Inspector, set the width of the view to 300 points (Figure 3-4).

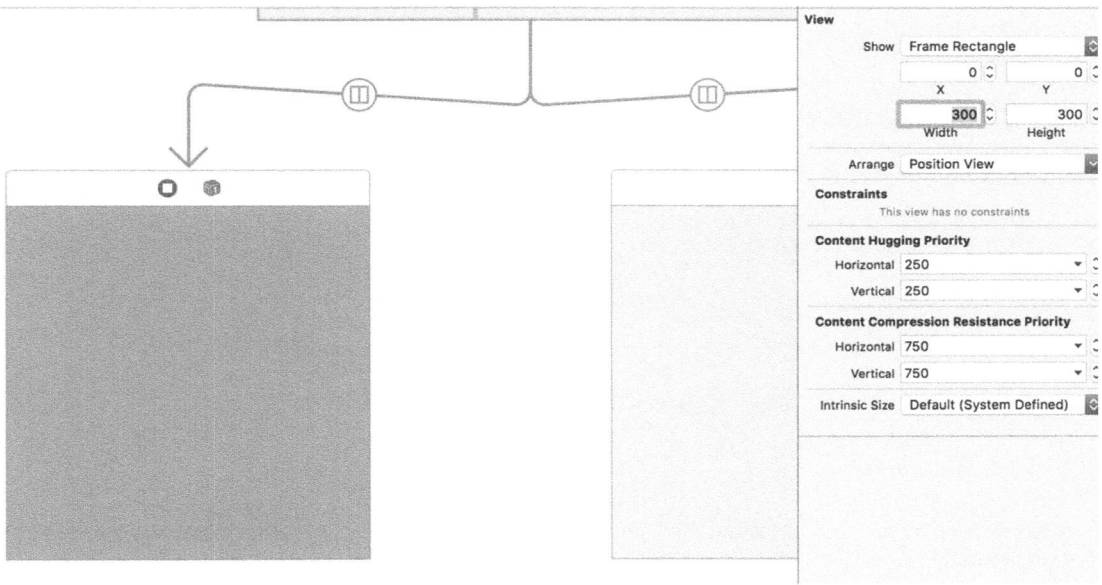

**Figure 3-4.** *Updating the sidebar's width*

Now we can drag a button image onto the sidebar. Set the button's title to be "New Park" using the Attributes Inspector. Using the Size Inspector, set the width of the button to 258 points and the height to 50. Position the button 40 points from the top and 21 points from each side of the sidebar. To accomplish this, select the button on the storyboard and hold down the Option key (the same process as used in Sketch 3) with your mouse hovering over the parent view of the sidebar. Then use the arrow keys to move the button into place. Running the app now would still not show the window as you expected, but we are going to fix that next. If you are wondering where I am getting all these "magic" numbers from, I am taking them directly from our sketch mockup.

Now we must add constraints to our new button. With the button selected, use the "Align button" option to align it horizontally in the container (Figure 3-5).

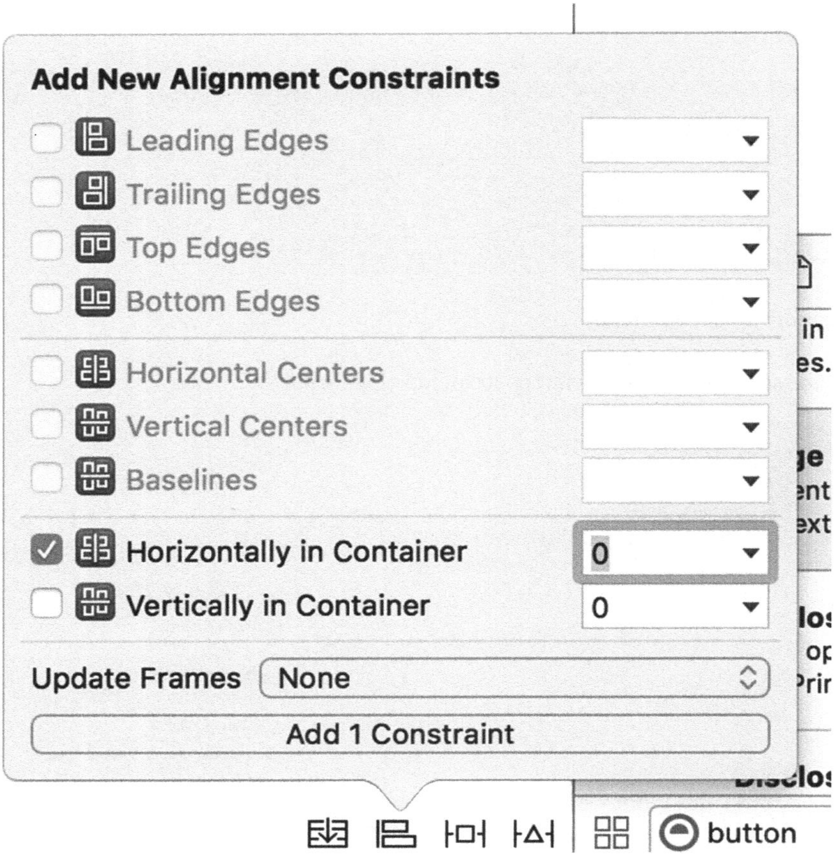

*Figure 3-5. Alignment constraints*

Xcode is going to complain about the Y position needing a constraint, so let's fix that now. Use the Pin button to pin the New Park button 40 points from the top of the sidebar, 21 from left, and 21 from right. Also check the boxes for width and height; otherwise, the frame of the button could change to a size we don't want (Figure 3-6).

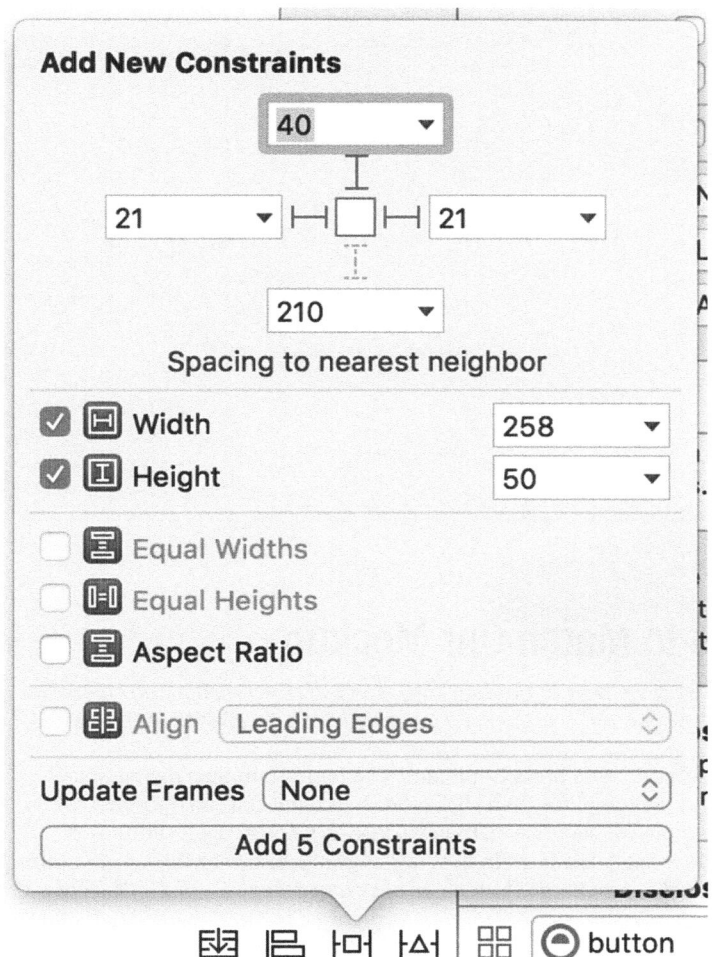

*Figure 3-6. Pin constraints*

Now there shouldn't be any complaints from Xcode. Run the project, and if all goes well you will now see the window correctly. See Figure 3-7.

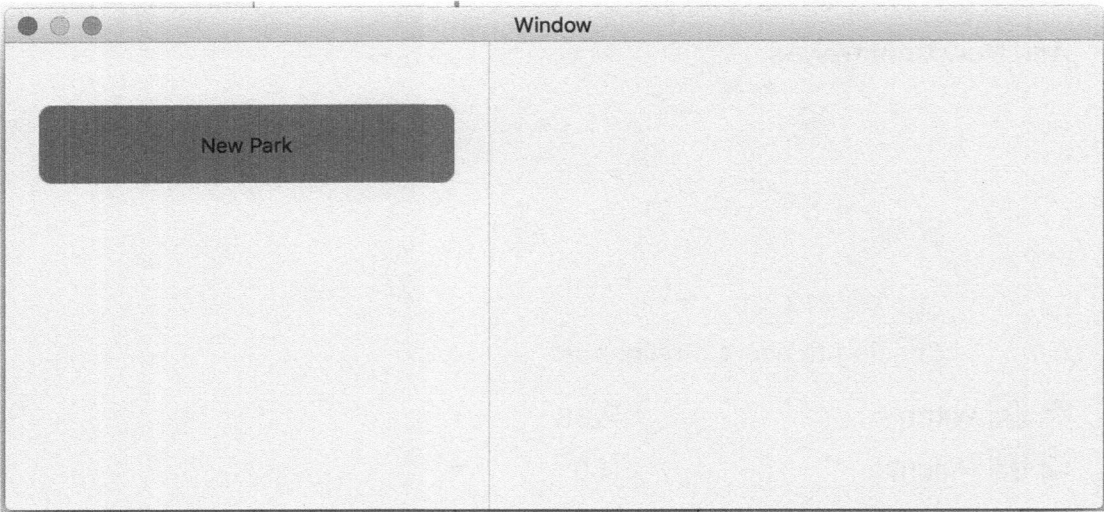

*Figure 3-7.* *The running app*

# Fixing the App's Colors to Match Our Mockup

The current running app doesn't match what we have in our mockup, especially the title bar and colors. We will fix that now. In order to change the title bar, we have to create our own subclass called NSWindow so we can override some settings.

Select the DogParks folder in the Navigator, then press Command + N. In the Template dialog, select "Source" under OS X and "Cocoa Class" as the template, then click Next. Name the class MainWindow, with subclass NSWindow, and make sure the language is set to Swift, then click Next. Choose the location you where you want to save the file, making sure DogParks is set in the Targets group, and click the Create button.

Now we want to override the initWithContentRect:styleMask:backing:defer: method (Objective-C format, as found in the Apple documentation), which allows us to change the style. We first need to make sure we call super.init so that all required initialization is completed before we make our changes. Next, we want to change the titleVisibility, titlebarAppearsTransparent, and styleMask. We also must implement the required init?(coder:) method to prevent getting an error in Xcode. Update the MainWindow.swift file with the code found in Listing 3-1.

*Listing 3-1.* Code for the Main Window

```
import Cocoa

class MainWindow: NSWindow {

    override init(contentRect: NSRect, styleMask aStyle: Int, backing bufferingType:
    NSBackingStoreType, `defer` flag: Bool) {

        super.init(contentRect: contentRect, styleMask: aStyle, backing: bufferingType,
        `defer`: flag)
```

```
        self.titleVisibility = NSWindowTitleVisibility.Hidden
        self.titlebarAppearsTransparent = true
        self.styleMask |= NSFullSizeContentViewWindowMask

    }

    required init?(coder: NSCoder) {
        fatalError("init(coder:) has not been implemented")
    }
}
```

The titleVisibility is a property used to control the window's title and title bar buttons' visibility. The available options for this property are NSWindowTitleVisibility.Visible or NSWindowTitleVisibility.Hidden.

The titleBarAppearsTransparent is a Boolean that tells the window whether to draw the title bar's background or not.

Finally, styleMask is used to determine what kinds of control items are displayed. The available options are shown in Listing 3-2.

**Listing 3-2.** Available Options for styleMask

```
var NSBorderlessWindowMask: Int { get }
var NSTitledWindowMask: Int { get }
var NSClosableWindowMask: Int { get }
var NSMiniaturizableWindowMask: Int { get }
var NSResizableWindowMask: Int { get }
var NSTexturedBackgroundWindowMask: Int { get }
var NSUnifiedTitleAndToolbarWindowMask: Int { get }
var NSFullScreenWindowMask: Int { get }
var NSFullSizeContentViewWindowMask: Int { get }
```

Now, let's go back to Main.storyboard and update the window so it uses our subclass. Select the window, then update the class to MainWindow in the Identity Inspector (Figure 3-8).

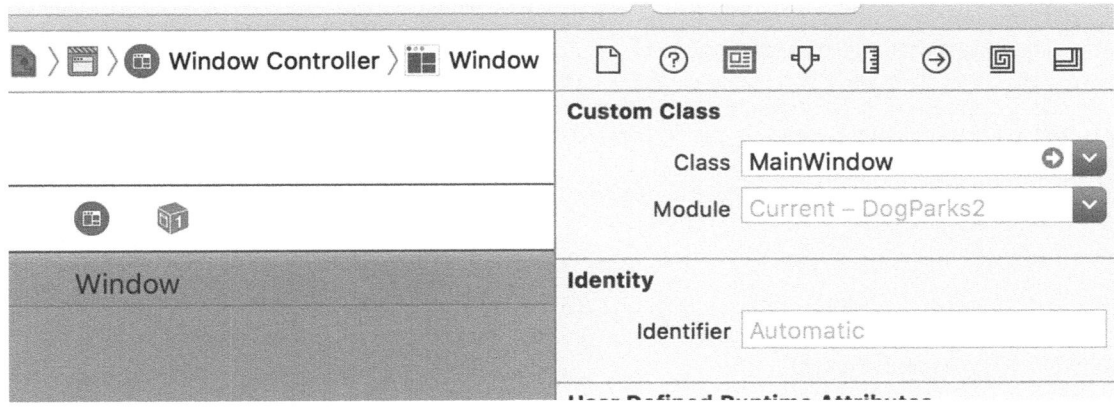

**Figure 3-8.** *Class set to our custom MainWindow*

Let's build and run the app to see what we were able to change. We see the title bar is a lot closer to what we had in our mockup (see Figure 3-9). Next, we will update the sidebar's color to match what we created in Sketch 3.

**Figure 3-9.** *Running app with updated title bar*

Repeat the steps you just followed to create a custom class. Name the class ParkListViewController and create subclass NSViewController. Make sure Swift is selected as the language and that the checkbox for creating a NIB is unchecked.

Sketch provides us with easy access to a hex value for the color; however, the CGColorRef that we will be using does not provide a way to use hex codes, so we are going to create two helper methods.

Open the AppDelegate.swift file. At the bottom, outside of the class definition, add the following function. We are putting this in the AppDelegate only, because we will be using it in multiple places (Listing 3-3).

**Listing 3-3.** Helper Methods for Creating a Color from a Hex Value

```
func CGColorCreateWithHexValues(red red: Int, green: Int, blue: Int) -> CGColor {
    assert(red >= 0 && red <= 255, "Invalid red component")
    assert(green >= 0 && green <= 255, "Invalid green component")
    assert(blue >= 0 && blue <= 255, "Invalid blue component")

    return CGColorCreateGenericRGB(CGFloat(red) / 255.0, CGFloat(green) / 255.0,
CGFloat(blue) / 255.0, 1.0)
}

func CGColorCreateFromHex(netHex: Int) -> CGColor {
    return CGColorCreateWithHexValues(red: (netHex >> 16) & 0xff, green:(netHex >> 8)
& 0xff, blue:netHex & 0xff)
}
```

This will allow us to easily set colors using hex values, which are the standard, especially if you have experience with web development.

Let's go back to ParkListViewController and use one of our new methods to set the background color of the sidebar. We are going to have to override awakeFromNib and set the view.layer?.backgroundColor. Update your class to look like the following (Listing 3-4).

*Listing 3-4.* Initial ParkListViewController

```
import Cocoa

class ParkListViewController: NSViewController {

    override func viewDidLoad() {
        super.viewDidLoad()
        // Do view setup here.
    }

    override func awakeFromNib() {
        if self.view.layer != nil {
            let color : CGColorRef = CGColorCreateFromHex(0xF5F7F7)
            self.view.layer?.backgroundColor = color
        }
    }
}
```

We first check to make sure that the view.layer has actually been created. Next, we use our new method to create a color from the hex value we get from Sketch. In Sketch, when you click on the color box inside the popup, you see the hex value. Just make sure when using that value with this method you append it with 0x (Zero), so in our case it is 0xF5F7F7 (see Figure 3-10).

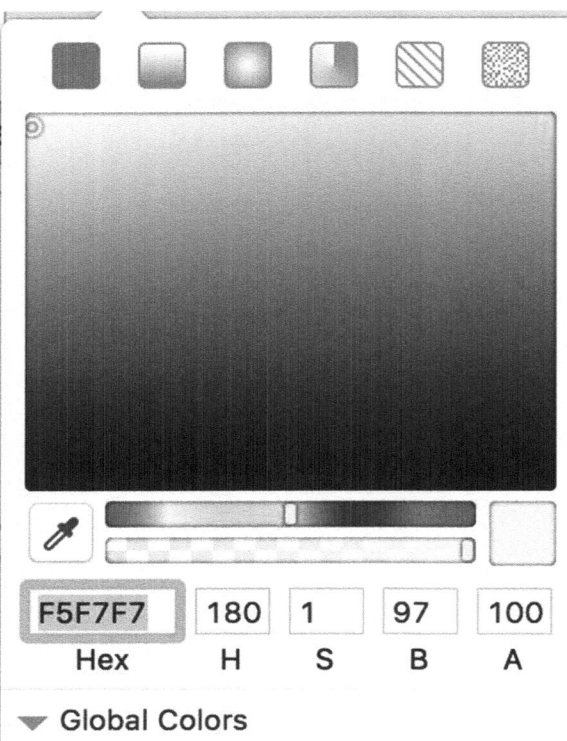

**Figure 3-10.** *The color picker*

Finally, we set the `view.layer?.backgroundColor` to the new color we just created. If you build and run the application now, you will see the sidebar with the new color (Figure 3-11).

**Figure 3-11.** *The app with the updated sidebar color*

Next, we need to make a final change to our button by updating the text size and font color. We are able to use Interface Builder to update the font type and size; however, we are unable to update the font color for the NSButton. This means we are going to have to write some custom code to accomplish this.

First, we must create an outlet for our button. Open the Main.storyboard and select the sidebar, then open the Assistant Editor. Finally, press Control and click and drag the sidebar to the ParkListViewController.swift file above the viewDidLoad method, then release your mouse. In the dialog, make sure "outlet" is selected and name it newParkButton.

Update the viewDidLoad method so it looks like the code in Listing 3-5.

*Listing 3-5.* Code to Update the New Park Button Title, Font, and Size

```
override func viewDidLoad() {
        super.viewDidLoad()

        let style = NSMutableParagraphStyle()
        style.alignment = .Center

        newParkButton.attributedTitle = NSAttributedString(string: "New Park", attributes:
[ NSForegroundColorAttributeName : NSColor.whiteColor(), NSParagraphStyleAttributeName :
style, NSFontAttributeName: NSFont(name: "Helvetica Neue", size: 20)!])
    }
```

Because we are going to be overriding the button's attributedTitle we must set everything–including alignment–in code. We use an NSMutableParagraphStyle to handle setting the alignment to Center. Next, we create a new NSAttributedString with the title "New Park" and use it to set the color and paragraph style, and we use the font attribute name to set the font and the font size.

To learn more about attributed strings, review the *Attributed String Programming Guide* for details about which attributes you can use. View the "Standard Attributes" section of the guide here:
https://developer.apple.com/library/mac/documentation/Cocoa/Conceptual/AttributedStrings/
AttributedStrings.html

Run the app to see the New Park button with the size and style that match our mockup. See Figure 3-12.

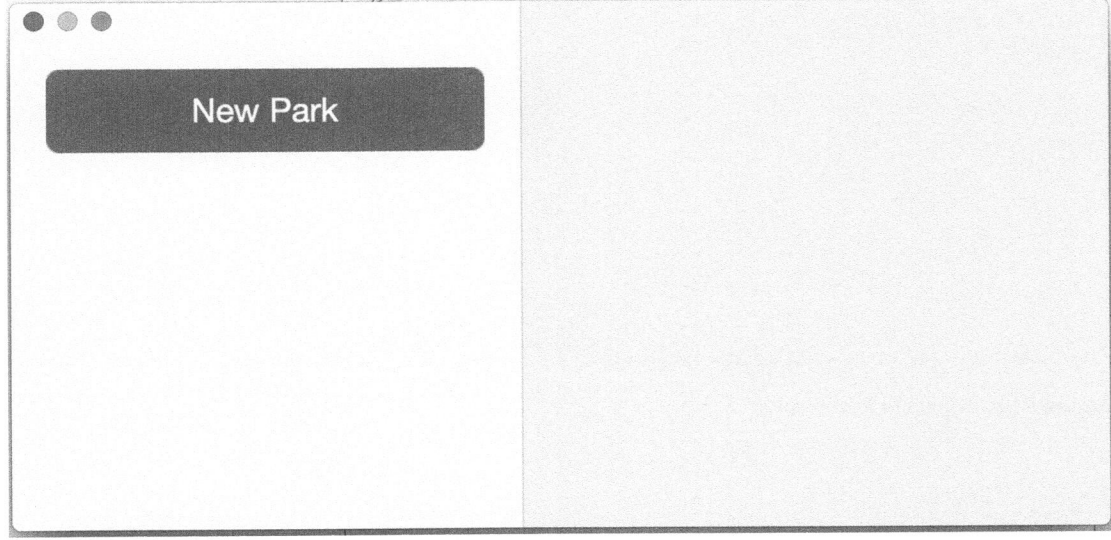

*Figure 3-12.* App with updated button text and style

A final optional task for the button is to set an alternative image background that is to be used when the button is clicked. By default, it will just darken the current light blue.

It is important to note that sometimes when running the app you will only see the sidebar. This is because we have not yet set the autolayout constraints for the details area of our app. We will handle this in a later section of this chapter.

# Adding the Search Box

Next, let's add the Search box. However, we will not be adding the search functionality at this stage. Before we do anything, let's adjust the height of our sidebar to match what we have in our mockup. Select the Sidebar View, then set the height to 500 points in the Size Inspector.

Find the Search field in the Object Library and drag it under the New Park button. In the Size Inspector, set its size to a width of 258 points, but notice that we cannot adjust the height. If we want to adjust the height, we must do so with a constraint. For this example we will leave the default height to acknowledge that once in a while a specific design feature from a mockup might not fit with what Xcode offers.

Position the Search box 18 points below the button and 21 points from both the left and right sidebar edges. (Hold down the Option key to see the guides.)

In the Attributes Inspector for the Search field, set the placeholder text to "Search for a Park." Next, we are going to set up the constraints for the Search field. In the Pin popup, select the top (18), left (21), right (21), and height checkboxes. Finally, click "Add constraints."

When running the app, you should see the output in Figure 3-13. Notice that the height doesn't match what we set in the storyboard. This is because we don't have any constraints set for the height. We will fix that in the next section when we add our Table View for the parks list.

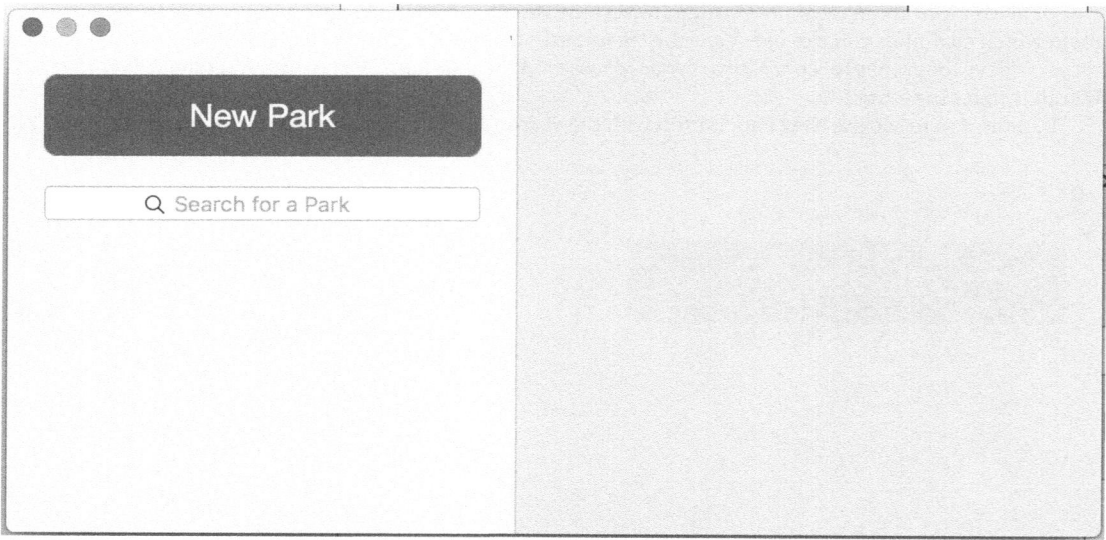

***Figure 3-13.*** *App with Search field*

# Implementing the Parks List

Drag a Table View from the Object Library and place it under the Search field. Make sure the top of the Table View is 18 points below the Search field. Next, drag the resize widgets to make the Table View take up the remaining bottom portion of the sidebar, and ensure that it is snug against both sides. In the Size Inspector, you should see a Table View width of 300 and height of 352.

In the Document Outliner, expand both the Bordered Scroll View and the Clip View, then select the Table View. In the Attributes Inspector, set the columns to 1 and uncheck the "Headers" checkbox. Select the Scroll View and then select the first option for the Border Type. With the Scroll View still selected, use the Pin dialog to add constraints for Top, Left, Right, Bottom, Height, and Width, then click "Add constraints."

Select the Table View in the Document Outliner again and set its background color to F5F7F7–the same color we used for the sidebar. If you now run the app you will notice the height of the sidebar has changed, and if you set the color correctly you shouldn't even notice the table (Figure 3-14).

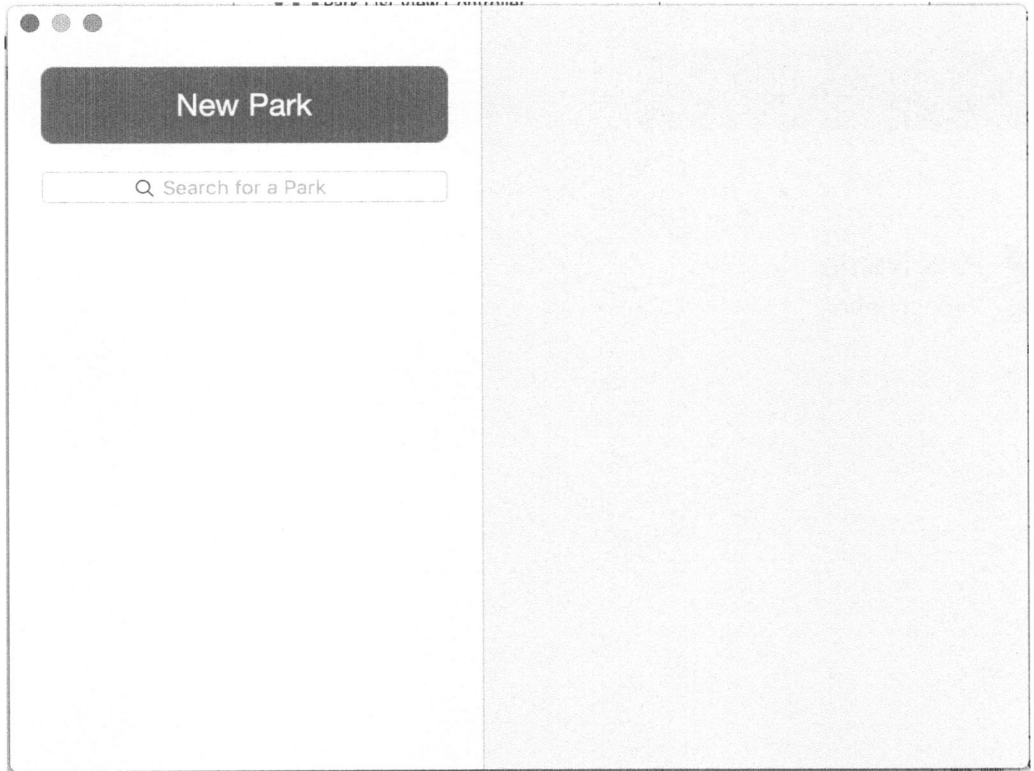

***Figure 3-14.*** *App with a Table View you can't see*

Next, we are going to adjust the size of our prototype cell. We will also add an Image View and another label. First, in the Document Outliner, drill down and select Table Cell View, then in the Size Inspector set its height to 72 points.

Let's now update the settings and location for the label that is currently in the cell. Select the Table View Cell and, still in the Size Inspector, change its height to 24 and its width to 217, then set x to 70 and y to 36. Next, change the font size to 20 in the Attributes Inspector. Change the label's title to Park Name as well.

Press the Option key and click and drag the Park Name label down to create a duplicate of it. In the Attributes Inspector, change the font size to 16. In the Size Inspector, set x to 70, y to 12, width to 217, and the height to 19. Change the label's title to Park Location.

Next, we will add an Image View to hold our park image. In the Object Library, find and drag an Image View to the left of the two labels. In the Size Inspector, update the view's x value to 12, y to 12, width to 48, and height to 48. We are going to want to set a placeholder image for now to give us an idea of what our cell will look like. Find an image of your choice and drag it into the Assets.xcassets so we can easily access it from the Attributes Inspector. I will be using the Ambleside picture. I set the Image setting to ambleside.jpg and changed the scaling to "Axes Independently." When finished, your sidebar should look like that in Figure 3-15.

**Figure 3-15.** *Shows the prototype Table View cell*

If you were to run the application now, you still would not see anything showing up for the park lists. This is because we have just created a prototype cell. Later, we will use bindings to actually display our list. For now, let's move on to the Detail View.

# Setting Up the Detail View

To get started, we need to create another subclass like we did for the sidebar. Create a new Cocoa Class named `DetailViewController` that inherits `NSViewController`, and make sure the option to create a NIB is not checked, and of course that the language is set to Swift.

The first thing we will take care of is the background color so that it matches our mockup. This requires us to do exactly what we did with the sidebar, with the exception, of course, of the color used. Override `awakeFromNib` and set the layer's background color to `0xFFFFFF`. When finished, `DetailViewController.swift` should contain the code shown in Listing 3-6.

*Listing 3-6.* Code for the Initial DetailViewController

```
import Cocoa

class DetailViewController: NSViewController {

    override func viewDidLoad() {
        super.viewDidLoad()
        // Do view setup here.
    }

    override func awakeFromNib() {
        if self.view.layer != nil {
            let color : CGColorRef = CGColorCreateFromHex(0xFFFFFF)
            self.view.layer?.backgroundColor = color
        }
    }
}
```

In the `Main.storyboard`, update the view controller that will be used for the park details so its class is set to `DetailViewController` in the Identity Inspector. When you run the project your window should now look like Figure 3-16.

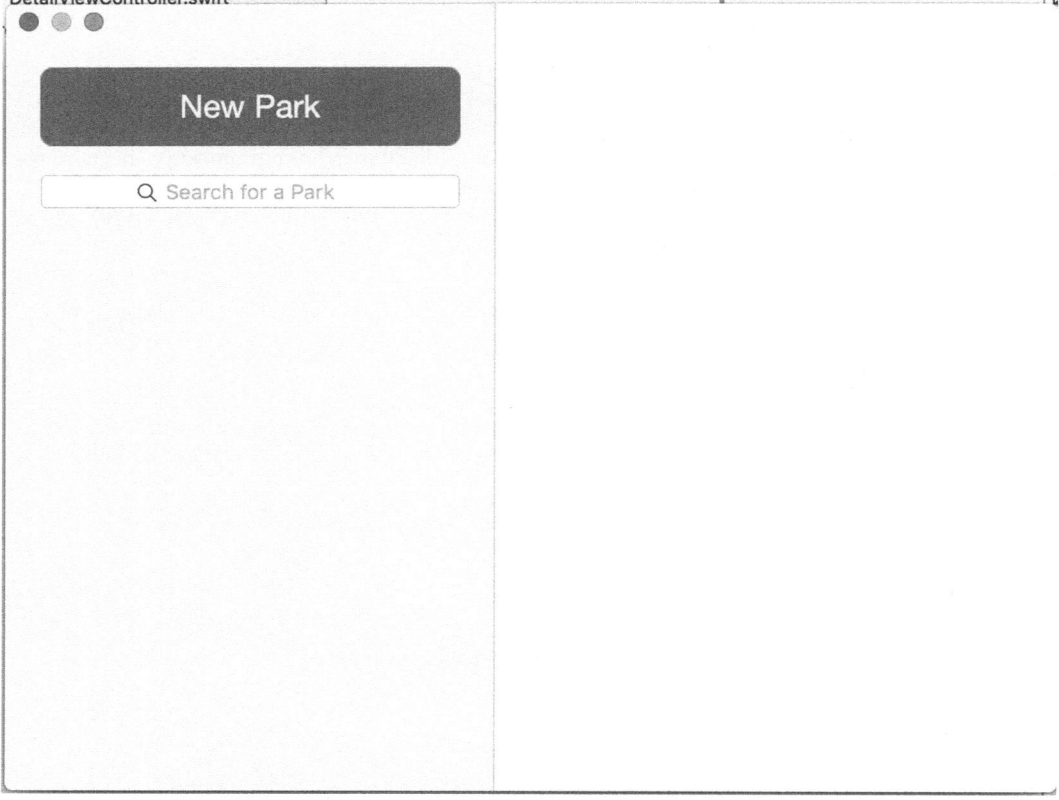

***Figure 3-16.*** *Detail view controller with a white background*

In the Size Inspector for the detail view controller, set both the width and height to 500.

Let's take a look at the detail part of our mockup for a refresher of what we are trying to accomplish (Figure 3-17).

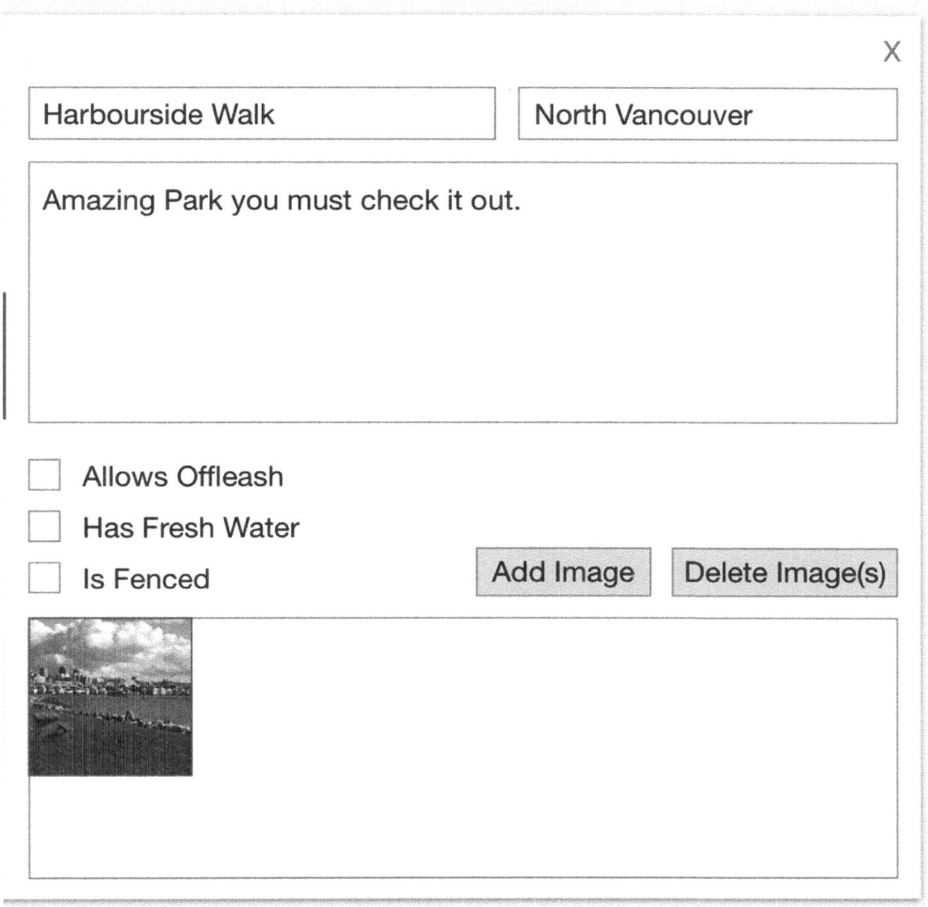

**Figure 3-17.** *Park details section of our mockup*

Based on this screenshot, we are going to need a Delete button, two text fields, a wrapping text field or Text View, three checkboxes, a button for adding an image, a button for deleting an image, and finally a Collection View to hold our images.

Let's start by dragging two text fields onto the detail view controller. Set the first text field (the one on the left) to be 40 points from the top, and make sure it snaps to the blue guideline on the left, which will place it 20 points from the left. Using the Size Inspector, set its width to 256 points.

Select the second text field and make sure it too is 40 points from the top. Set it to have a width of 192 and to rest against the right guideline. If you run the app now, you will see that the textbox on the right is cut off; to fix this we must add some constraints.

Select the first text field and use the Pin menu to add constraints for the top, left, right (distance to the second text field), width, and height. Select the second text field and use the Pin menu to add constraints for the top, left (distance to the first text field), width, and height. Finally, set the placeholder text for the first text field to "Park Name", and the placeholder text for the second text field to "Park Location". Now run the app; you will see the window correctly showing the text fields. See Figure 3-18.

**Figure 3-18.** *Park details section with park name and location text fields*

Drag a Text View from the Object Library and place it 18 points below the name/location text fields. Use the Pin menu to add constraints for top, left, right, and height.

Drag three checkboxes under the Text View. Set all the states to off. Change the title of the first one to "Allows Offleash", the second one to "Has Fresh Water", and the final one to "Is Fenced". You are going to have to use the resizing widgets on the storyboard to make sure all the text shows. Position the first checkbox 20 points below the Text View. Set the second one 10 points below the "Allows Offleash" checkbox, and set the last one 10 points below the "Has Fresh Water" checkbox.

Pin each of the checkboxes one by one using constraints for top, left, and width.

Now, drag a Collection View to the bottom of the Detail View. Set the height to 164 points. Finally, position the Collection View 20 points from the bottom, left, and right of the Detail View. Pin the Collection View to the top ("Is Fenced" checkbox), right, left, and bottom using constraints.

Unfortunately, there is a bug in Xcode with Collection Views and how Collection View items are created on the storyboard. If you try to run the application now, you will receive an error: "Unknown segue relationship: Prototype" (Figure 3-19).

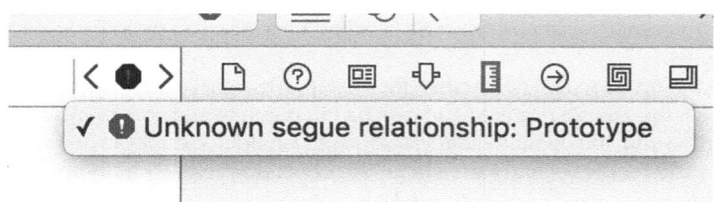

**Figure 3-19.** *Prototype Collection View item error*

Delete the segue between the Collection View and the Collection View items. This will get rid of the error, and when you run the app you will see the output shown in Figure 3-20.

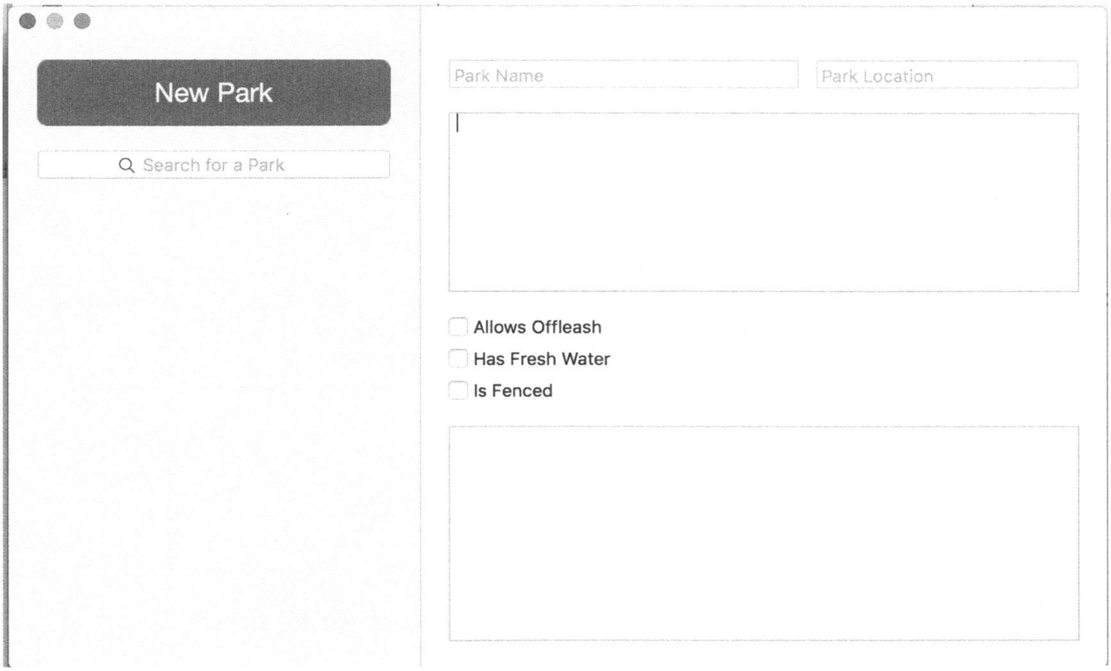

**Figure 3-20.** *Current app with Details View progress*

Let's add our last three buttons and then move on to fixing our Collection View. Drag two push buttons above the Collection View. Set the title of the button on the right to "Delete Image(s)", and set the title of the button on the left to "Add Image(s)". Set the position of the Delete Image(s) button to be 20 points from the right edge of the Detail View and 12 points above the Collection View. Set the position of the Add Image(s) button to be 12 points to the left of the Delete Image(s) button and 12 points above the Collection View. Using the Pin menu, add constraints for the Delete Image(s) button for the right, bottom, and left. Next, add constraints for the Add Image(s) button on the right and bottom.

Drag one more button and place it above the Park Location text field. This will be used to delete the park entry. Set the title to "Delete Park". (This is changed from the initial mockup to make it clear what this button does). Pin the button to the top, right, and bottom using constraints. When you are finished, your view should look like Figure 3-21.

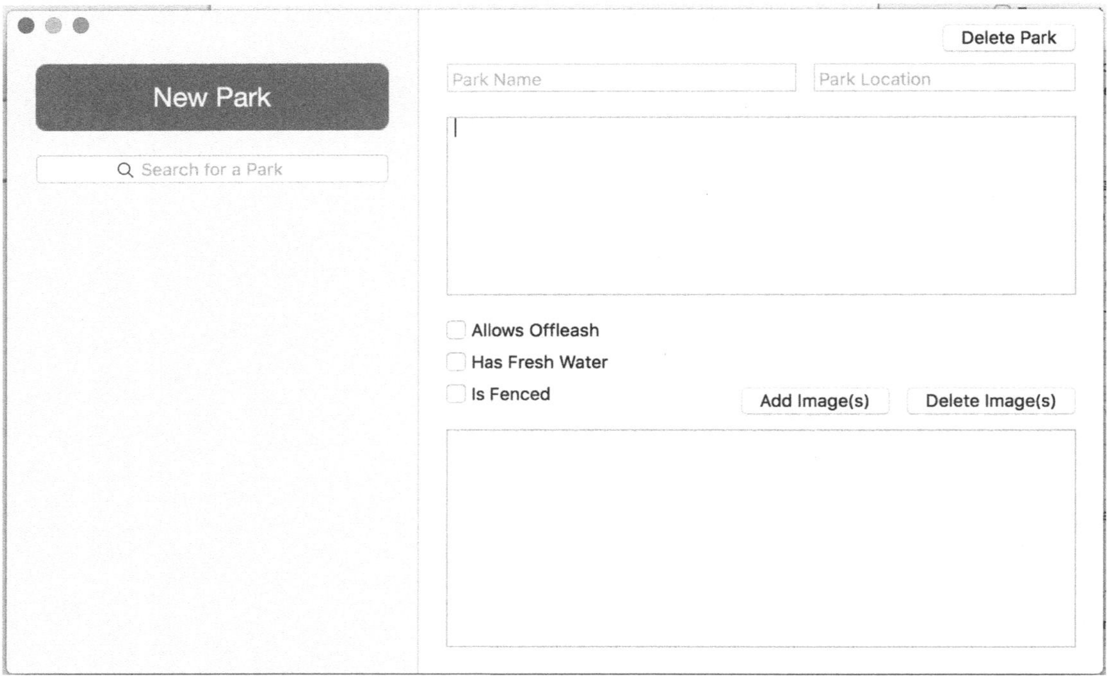

***Figure 3-21.*** *Park details section buttons for adding/deleteing images and deleting the park*

# Fixing the Collection View Item

First, we need to set the Storyboard ID in the Identity Inspector for the Collection View item to collectionViewItem. Next, let's adjust the size of the Items View where images will appear. Click inside the Collection View item or use the Document Outliner to select the view, then use the Size Inspector to change the width and height to 90.

Drag an Image View inside the Collection View item and use the size widgets to make the Image View fill the entire Collection View item area. Pin the Image View to the top (0), right (0), left (0), and bottom (0).

Open the DetailViewController.swift file. We are going to update the viewDidLoad function to link the Collection View to the Collection View item. We are also going to need an outlet to the Collection View. Update your DetailViewController to look like Listing 3-7.

***Listing 3-7.*** Code Connecting Collection Prototype Item to Collection View

```
import Cocoa

class DetailViewController: NSViewController {

    @IBOutlet weak var parkImagesCollection: NSCollectionView!

    override func viewDidLoad() {
        super.viewDidLoad()
```

```
        // don't forget to set identifier of collectionViewItem
        // from interface builder
        let itemPrototype = self.storyboard?.instantiateControllerWithIdentifier
            ("collectionViewItem")
            as! NSCollectionViewItem
        self.parkImagesCollection.itemPrototype = itemPrototype
    }

    override func awakeFromNib() {
        if self.view.layer != nil {
            let color : CGColorRef = CGColorCreateFromHex(0xFFFFFF)
            self.view.layer?.backgroundColor = color
        }
    }
}
```

If you try to run the app now, you will get an error because we have not connected the parkImagesCollection outlet to the view controller. Let's do that now. Open the main storyboard, open the Document Outliner, then select the collection view controller on the storyboard. This will then show the Bordered Scroll View. Expand this until you can see Collection View. Then press Control and click and drag from the detail view controller to the Collection View. In the popup window, select parkImagesCollection (Figure 3-22).

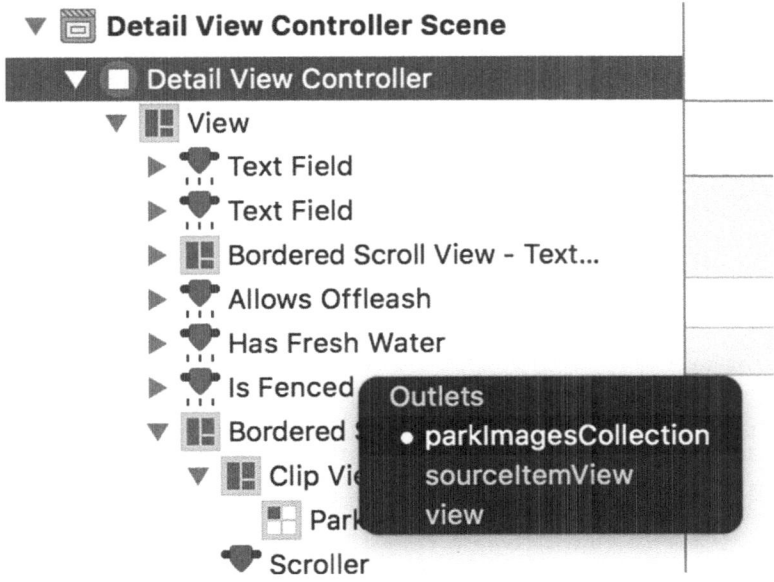

***Figure 3-22.*** *Connecting Collection View to parkImagesCollection outlet*

Now you should be able to build and run the app without any problems. At this point we have our prototype running in Xcode.

## Conclusion

This chapter enabled us to analyze the data we are going to need, which we will start working with in the next chapter. Then we went through the process of integrating our mockup in Xcode to create a prototype. In the next chapter, we will shift our focus over to CloudKit, where we will implement more functionality into our app as we learn about it.

# CHAPTER 4

# Introduction to CloudKit

Now that we know what data our app must store, we will take a look at CloudKit and how it can help meet our data-storage needs. In this chapter we will provide an overview of CloudKit at a high level and provide a walkthrough of the CloudKit Dashboard. This is where we will manage the application's data, configure access rights, and monitor resource usage.

## iCloud Accounts

iCloud accounts are the backbone of CloudKit. Anything you do requires a logged-in account, with the exception of browsing public data (which will be discussed later). This gives us the benefit of having access to hundreds of millions of users without needing to develop our own authentication layer. In addition, iCloud accounts and CloudKit work seamlessly together, so if the end user is already logged in to their iCloud account they will not be asked to log in to the app. They can just start using it and creating records.

## Containers

CloudKit–like most Apple technologies–revolves around the concept of containers. Containers provide a way for apps to be uniquely identified. With CloudKit, you always have one default container; additionally, your app can access other containers to which you give it access. Being able to access additional containers enables the sharing of data between apps, so we can have an OS X admin/management app to control business-related data and a public iOS app that accesses the data as read only. The default container is the same thing as the bundle identifier. It is very important to remember that once a CloudKit container is created it *cannot be deleted,* so make sure your bundle identifier is what you plan to use permanently. Containers must be unique across all developers. A good practice while you are learning CloudKit is to pick one identifier you will use for all your test apps. Then, whenever you want to create a new app using that identifier, reset the development environment through the CloudKit Dashboard. (We will cover this later.)

Think of a container as a sandbox that only your app can access. Every app that uses CloudKit has its own sandbox. This prevents apps from overriding each other's data, and ensures your data stays secure and other developers cannot ever get access to it.

Containers are exposed as a CKContainer:

```
let container = CKContainer.defaultContainer()
```

© Bruce Wade 2016

B. Wade, *OS X App Development with CloudKit and Swift*, DOI 10.1007/978-1-4842-1880-8_4

# Databases

CloudKit provides us with access to two different databases, a public database that every client app has access to, and a private database that only the account that is being used to access CloudKit can access. It is important to remember that we as developers cannot access the private database of an end user. Public database resource costs go against the developer's quota, whereas the private database resource costs go against the end user's iCloud data.

In the case of the Parks app, we will be storing our data in the public database so other users are able to view it. Although we won't be using the private database in this book, we should go over some use cases to give you an example of when to use the private rather than the public database.

If we wanted to add functionality for the user to create private notes about a given park–for warnings or reminders to themselves–we would store this information in the user's private database, as other members don't need to know about these. However, if we wanted to create an event on a specific date for a park meetup, that information would go in the public database so other members could view it and join.

Databases are exposed as a CKDatabase. You get access to the databases through the CKContainer:

```
let publicDatabase = CKContainer.defaultContainer().publicCloudDatabase
let privateDatabase = CKContainer.defaultContainer().privateCloudDatabase
```

You can create access roles and permissions for public databases in the CloudKit Dashboard.

# Records

A CKRecord is structure data that wraps key-value pairs, where each value has a record type. A record in the developer mode uses a just-in-time schema. When you move to production, the data is not used as just-in-time. This means while you are developing your app you can change your data structure as much as you want. However once your app is moved into the production database you can no longer change the data structure.

The supported record types are NSString, NSNumber, NSData, NSDate, CLLocation, CKReference, CKAsset; a record can also be an array instead of a single record type (Listing 4-1).

**Listing 4-1.** Different Ways of Getting and Setting CKRecord Values

```
let park = CKRecord(recordType: "Park")
// Setting values
park.setObject("Lafarge Lake", forKey: "name")
park["location"] = "Vancouver, BC"

// Accessing values
var name = park.objectForKey("name")
var location = park["location"]
```

## Record Zones

Records are grouped within record zones. There can be multiple record zones. Every container has a default record zone.

## Record Identifiers

CKRecordID contains a recordName and CKRecordZoneID. If you don't provide a CKRecordZoneID the default record zone will be used. If you don't provide a recordName a default one will be created for you.

# References

CKReference allows you to relate CKRecords with each other. When creating references you should use back references; for example, park images should have a reference to their parent, instead of the park having a list of images. References can be set to cascade delete, so if a park is deleted all related images are also deleted at the same time.

# Assets

CKAssets are used to store large files such as images or videos and are stored as bulk storage. CloudKit takes care of efficiently uploading and downloading assets for you. Assets are owned by CKRecords and are transferred as files on disk. See Listing 4-2.

***Listing 4-2.*** Add an Asset to a CKRecord

```
let photoURL = NSURL(fileURLWithPath: "...")
let parkThumbnail = CKAsset(fileURL: photoURL)
park["thumbnail"] = parkThumbnail
```

# Convenience API

You can save a record using saveRecord with the completionHandler call on either the public or private databases. This is an asynchronous method call, so make sure to handle errors, as this can be the difference between a functional and non-functional app. See Listing 4-3.

***Listing 4-3.*** Code for Saving a Record

```
// Create a record ID or allow CloudKit to create a
// random one for you.
let recordID = CKRecordID(recordName: "vanLostParkID")
// Create a new record using the RecordID if created
let park = CKRecord(recordType: "Park", recordID: recordID)
// Choose either the public or private database where you
// want to save the record
let publicDatabase = CKContainer.defaultContainer().publicCloudDatabase
// Use the convience API saveRecord with completionHandler
publicDatabase.saveRecord(park) { (savedPark: CKRecord?, error: NSError?) -> Void in
    // Handle any errors when error != nil
}
```

You can fetch a specific record using a predetermined CKRecordID and the fetchRecordWithID and completionHandler convenience API (Listing 4-4).

***Listing 4-4.*** How to Fetch a Record

```
// Fetching a record from CloudKit
// Use a predetermined CKRecordID
let recordID = CKRecordID(recordName: "vanLostParkID")
// Choose either the public or private database where
// you want to save the record
```

```
let publicDatabase = CKContainer.defaultContainer().publicCloudDatabase
// Use the convenience API fetchRecordWithID
// and completionHandler
publicDatabase.fetchRecordWithID(recordID) { (park: CKRecord?, error: NSError?) -> Void in
    // Handle any errors when error != nil
}
```

As shown in Listing 4-5, you can query a record, modify it, and then save it back to the server.

***Listing 4-5.*** How to Query a Record, Modify It, and Save It Back to CloudKit

```
// Fetching a record from CloudKit
// Use a predetermined CKRecordID
let recordID = CKRecordID(recordName: "vanLostParkID")
// Choose either the public or private database
// where you want to save the record
let publicDatabase = CKContainer.defaultContainer().publicCloudDatabase
// Use the convenience API fetchRecordWithID
// and completionHandler
publicDatabase.fetchRecordWithID(recordID) { (fetchedPark: CKRecord?, error: NSError?) ->
Void in
    // Handle any errors when error != nil
    if error != nil {} else {
      // Modify the fetched park
      fetchedPark!["name"] = "Updated Park Name"
      // Save the modified park back to CloudKit
      publicDatabase.saveRecord(fetchedPark!, completionHandler: {
      (savedPark: CKRecord?, error: NSError?) -> Void in
        // Handle any errors when error != nil
      })
    }
}
```

# Queries

CKQuery combines a RecordType, an NSPredicate, and NSSortDescriptors (optional) to give users a focused chunk of data to work with. CloudKit supports only subsets of the NSPredictate features. Queries are polls from the database; they should not be used for querying data that returns the same result sets over and over again. See Listing 4-6.

***Listing 4-6.*** Querying CloudKit Using a Predicate

```
let predicate = NSPredicate(format: "name = %@", "Updated Park Name")

let query = CKQuery(recordType: "Park", predicate: predicate)
let publicDatabase = CKContainer.defaultContainer().publicCloudDatabase

publicDatabase.performQuery(query, inZoneWithID: nil) {
(results: [CKRecord]?, error: NSError?) -> Void in
    // Handle errors
```

```
    if error == nil {
      for record in results! {
          print("\(record)")
      }
    }
}
```

# Subscriptions

CKSubcription combines a RecordType, an NSPredicate, and a Push. This allows the server to push any new changes to any devices listening instead of requiring the device to poll for changes (Listing 4-7).

*Listing 4-7.* Setting Up a Subscription

```
let publicDatabase = CKContainer.defaultContainer().publicCloudDatabase
let predicate = NSPredicate(format: "name = %@", "Updated Park Name")
// Send a push notification whenever the record(s)
// found from the predicate change
let subscription = CKSubscription(recordType: "Park", predicate: predicate,
options: CKSubscriptionOptions.FiresOnRecordUpdate)
// Tell the application how to handle the notification
let notificationInfo = CKNotificationInfo()
notificationInfo.alertLocalizationKey = "LOCAL_NOTIFICATION_KEY"
notificationInfo.soundName = "Park.aiff"
notificationInfo.shouldBadge = true
subscription.notificationInfo = notificationInfo

// Save the subscription to the server
publicDatabase.saveSubscription(subscription) { (subscription: CKSubscription?,
error: NSError?) -> Void in
    // Handle errors when error != nil
}

// Update application:didReceiveRemoteNotification
// to handle CloudKit notifcations
func application(application: NSApplication, didReceiveRemoteNotification userInfo:
[String : AnyObject]) {
    let cloudKitNotification = CKNotification(fromRemoteNotificationDictionary:
    userInfo as! [String: NSObject])
    let alertBody = cloudKitNotification.alertBody

    if cloudKitNotification.notificationType == CKNotificationType.Query {
      let queryNotification: CKQueryNotification = cloudKitNotification as!
      CKQueryNotification
      let recordID = queryNotification.recordID
    }
}
```

# CloudKit User Accounts

CloudKit user accounts provide a way to identify the user with metadata about the user. Any client talking to the same container will be returned the same ID for the logged-in user, regardless of whether the client is OS X, iOS, or web using CloudKitJS (Listing 4-8). You can also leverage this identity to uniquely interact with your own servers without requiring the user to log in.

***Listing 4-8.*** Getting the Current Logged-in User's Identifier

```
// This gets the current logged-in user's identifier CKContainer.defaultContainer().
fetchUserRecordIDWithCompletionHandler { (userRecordID: CKRecordID?, error: NSError?) ->
Void in
   // Handle errors when error != nil
}
```

Metadata allows us to set key-value pairs on a user record. User records in the public database are world readable (Listing 4-9). You cannot query user records.

***Listing 4-9.*** Getting Metadata about a User

```
let defaultContainer = CKContainer.defaultContainer()
let publicDatabase = defaultContainer.publicCloudDatabase
defaultContainer.fetchUserRecordIDWithCompletionHandler { (userRecordID: CKRecordID?,
error: NSError?) -> Void in
   // Handle errors when error != nil
   if error != nil {} else {
      // Get the user record from CloudKit using the
      // recordID for the logged-in user
      publicDatabase.fetchRecordWithID(userRecordID!, completionHandler: {
      (userRecord: CKRecord?, error: NSError?) -> Void in
         // Handle errors
         if error != nil {} else {
           // User records are like any other records; you
           // can add key-values and resave them to the
           // CloudKit database.
           // Assuming we have a displayname
           var displayName = userRecord!["displayName"]
           print("\(displayName)")
        }
      })
   }
}
```

For privacy reasons no personal identifying information is provided by default. You can request that information via CloudKit, and the user has to either accept or decline providing personal information.

User discovery allows you to gather information from the user if they have opted in to being discoverable. You can also leverage the address book to find any of your contacts that are also using the server, but they will have to enable discovery first (Listing 4-10). Leveraging the address book through CloudKit does not require the user to authorize you to access their address book; you are just accessing your own.

*Listing 4-10.* Using the Address Book to Find Information about Other Users

```
let defaultContainer = CKContainer.defaultContainer()
        defaultContainer.discoverAllContactUserInfosWithCompletionHandler {
        (userInfos: [CKDiscoveredUserInfo]?, error: NSError?) -> Void in
    // Handle errors
    if error != nil {} else {
        for userInfo in userInfos! {
            // familyName will only show if the user
            // has oped in to showing it.
            print("\(userInfo.userRecordID) \(userInfo.displayContact?.familyName)")
        }
    }
}
```

# CloudKit Dashboard

When you log in to `https://icloud.developer.apple.com/dashboard` you will be presented with the screen shown in Figure 4-1. Let's quickly go over what the Dashboard contains.

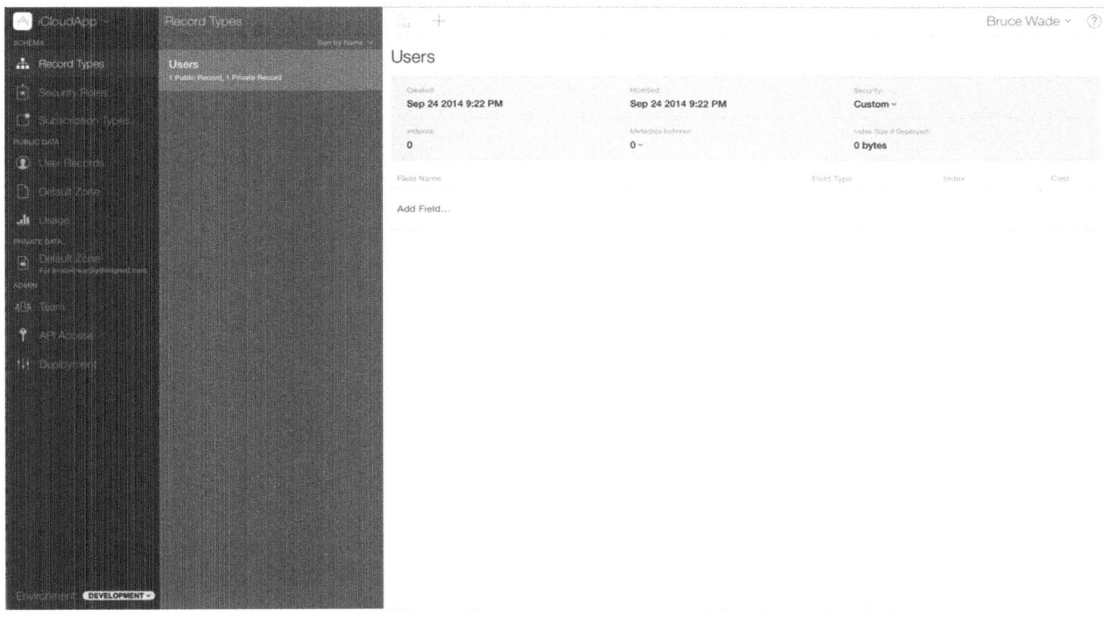

*Figure 4-1.* CloudKit Dashboard

First, in the top left-hand corner you will find a drop-down. This drop-down contains a list of all the app containers that you have enabled for CloudKit. When you select the one you want to work with, the page is updated to show the data in the selected container.

# Schema Record Types

The user's type represents a CloudKit-generated record type that cannot be deleted. You can, however, add additional fields to this record type. The User record type, as the name suggests, is used to store information about each user who has used your app.

When you select a record type from the Record Types column, the detail pane will update to show all fields related to the selected type. This is also where you can set metadata indexes and security settings for a given record type.

You can create a new type by clicking the + symbol at the top left-hand corner of the detail pane (Figure 4-2).

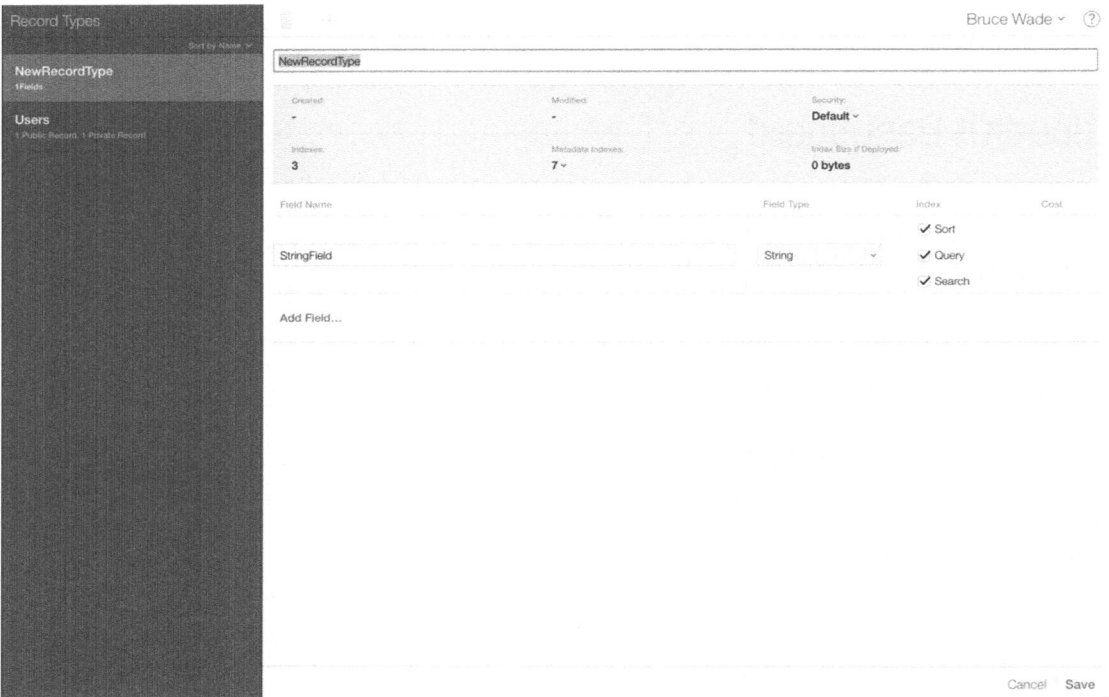

***Figure 4-2.*** *Creating a new record type*

You are then asked to name the new type. It is important to enter a name before you save, as you cannot change it once the type has been saved. Notice that the Created and Modified fields are automatically created for each record type; you cannot delete these fields. There is also a field automatically added, which you should change before saving. To add additional fields simply click the "Add Field..." link. You can either add all the fields when you are first creating the type, update them later, or when in development mode allow your app to dynamically add new ones through code. As you can see from Figure 4-3, there are several options for field type, which can either be a single entry or a list.

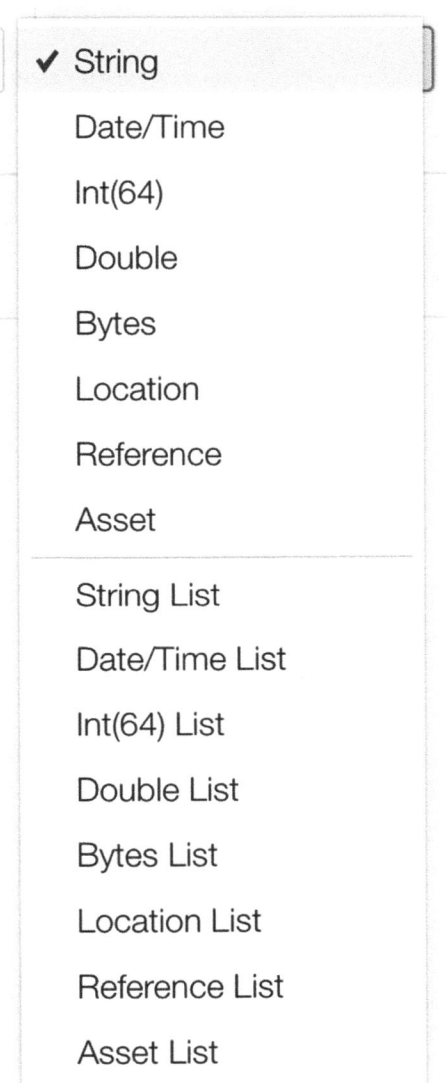

*Figure 4-3.* *List of the available field types*

Finally, you can set indexes for individual fields, which is important if you find your app is always querying a specific field of a record type.

If after you save you realize you do not want the new record type anymore, simply select the type from the list and click on the trashcan icon in the details pane to delete it. For the Users type, the trashcan is disabled because you are unable to delete this type.

If you have added a field you no longer wish to have, select the record type and hover the cursor over the field you wish to delete. In the cost column you will see an X; clicking on this deletes the field.

# Security Roles

The Security Roles section under Schema allows you to control who can update, create, and view different record types. This is a two-step process. First, you must create a security role. Second, you must add that role to the users to whom you wish to give those permissions.

By default there are no security roles created. To create a new one, click on the + sign in the detail pane. You are asked to name the role. Do so and click Save. Now you can assign permissions to the record types. You can add as many record type permissions as you want per security role, and you can give each security role permission to create, read, or write to a given record type (Figure 4-4).

***Figure 4-4.*** *New ParkManager security role*

We will cover how to assign these roles to a user once when we go over public data.

# Subscription Types

This section lists any subscription types that have been created. You can only view them in the Dashboard and cannot create them. They must be created in your app itself.

# Public Data User Records

If you haven't set any metadata indexes for a user record, you will see the following issue: "Records of this type cannot be shown because there is no Query Index of Record ID field." Below the message, click the link that says "Add Record ID Query Index." After that, any users that have used your app will show up. If the user has not shared their name, the record will display as No Name.

If you want to assign a user to a security role you have created, select the user in the list or search for the user by clicking the magnifying glass icon. Next, in the detail pane, select "Roles" from the drop-down under Security and check any roles you want this user to have (Figure 4-5).

**Figure 4-5.** *How to assign a security role to a user*

# Default Zone

The Default Zone shows all data that is in the public database. You need to use the drop-down in the second pane to select which record type you want to see data for. Once the data type is selected, the data for the record type will be displayed. When you select a row, the detail pane will show all the information for that record that can be edited or deleted. You can also create new rows for a record type by using the + icon in the detail pane. Finally, you can use the Search and Filter functionalities to narrow down the search results.

# Usage

The Usage section shows you how many resources your app is currently using and how close it is to the limit. It also shows a predictive forecast of how much your app might use the specified resources over time. Apple gives a generous number of free resources that increases as the number of app users increases. It is important to monitor this section to ensure you don't have any major bugs that are using resources, especially as regards requests per second.

# Private Data Default Zone

If you use your app with the same iCloud account as your CloudKit developer account uses, you will be able to see any private records for that user account here. Otherwise, if you use a second iCloud account, you will see an empty result set for all of the record types.

# Admin Team

This section lists all the members on your development team. You can enabled or disable privileges for each of them in regards to managing the team, edit development, and edit production. You can also view when a member last logged in, their name, and their Apple ID.

# API Access

In this section you can enable an access token that can be used with the CloudKitJS SDK to enable you to build web applications that interact with CloudKit. This is out of the scope of this book, and for those interested you should view the Apple WWDC videos related to the JS SDK.

# Deployment

The Deployment section allows you to reset the development environment, which will clear all data and delete all record types. This is also the place where you deploy your metadata to production. This will only move your schemas, not any of your development data. It is important to remember that once you deploy to production you will no longer be able to delete field types, so always make sure you have fully tested your app in development before moving it to production.

# Conclusion

This chapter has provided an overview of CloudKit, along with the CloudKit Dashboard. We mainly focused on the CloudKit convenience API; however, in later chapters we will be using the `NSOperations` CloudKit API.

For additional information on CloudKit, it is recommended that you watch all the WWDC videos (`https://developer.apple.com/videos/wwdc2015/`) related to CloudKit before moving on to the next chapter.

# CHAPTER 5

# Creating Test Data with CloudKit Dashboard

In this chapter we will take information about the data we created in chapter 3 and create record types using the CloudKit Dashboard. Next, we will use the Dashboard to create some test data that we will add to our prototype in the next chapter.

## Setting Up Our Project for CloudKit

In the previous chapter we took a look at CloudKit. However, when using the Dashboard our app was not listed in the container list. This is because we have not yet enabled CloudKit for our app. Let's do that now.

First, you must have a developer account, because only apps distributed to the App Store can use CloudKit, and you need a developer account to upload to the App Store.

Next, as was already emphasized, you cannot change or delete your container once it is created, so before following the steps to enable CloudKit, make sure your bundle identifier is set to a value you want to keep. Then click on the Capabilities tab and toggle the On/Off switch for iCloud (see Figure 5-1).

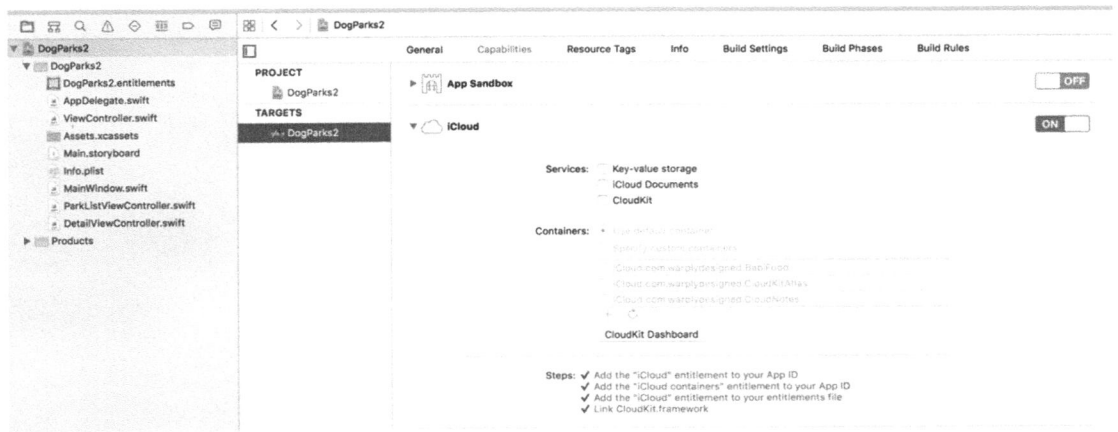

*Figure 5-1.* *Turning on iCloud*

© Bruce Wade 2016
B. Wade, *OS X App Development with CloudKit and Swift*, DOI 10.1007/978-1-4842-1880-8_5

You are going to want to enable key-value storage and CloudKit. Once you click CloudKit, your container will be created, so be sure to click the "Key-value storage" checkbox first. Now open CloudKit Dashboard by clicking the CloudKit Dashboard button, and you will see your app and container are ready for you to select and start adding data to.

## Goals of Test Data

The primary goal of using test data before doing any programming is to help us quickly think about what data we want to display and make available to the user, and what public data we want to control ourselves without allowing the general users to create, update, or delete it. Finally, probably the most important aspect is to give our application some real data to work with so we can test what happens when the network is slow, when there is no Internet connection, or when we change the data in a different place then in our app. (Do we get push notifications? Does our app automatically update to show the new data?)

## Creating the Parks Record Type

In the CloudKit Dashboard, make sure your app is selected from the top drop-down, and then select "Record Types" under Schema. You should only see the Users record type. In the detail pane click on the + icon to create a new record type, then name it Parks. Figure 5-2 shows the completed Parks record type.

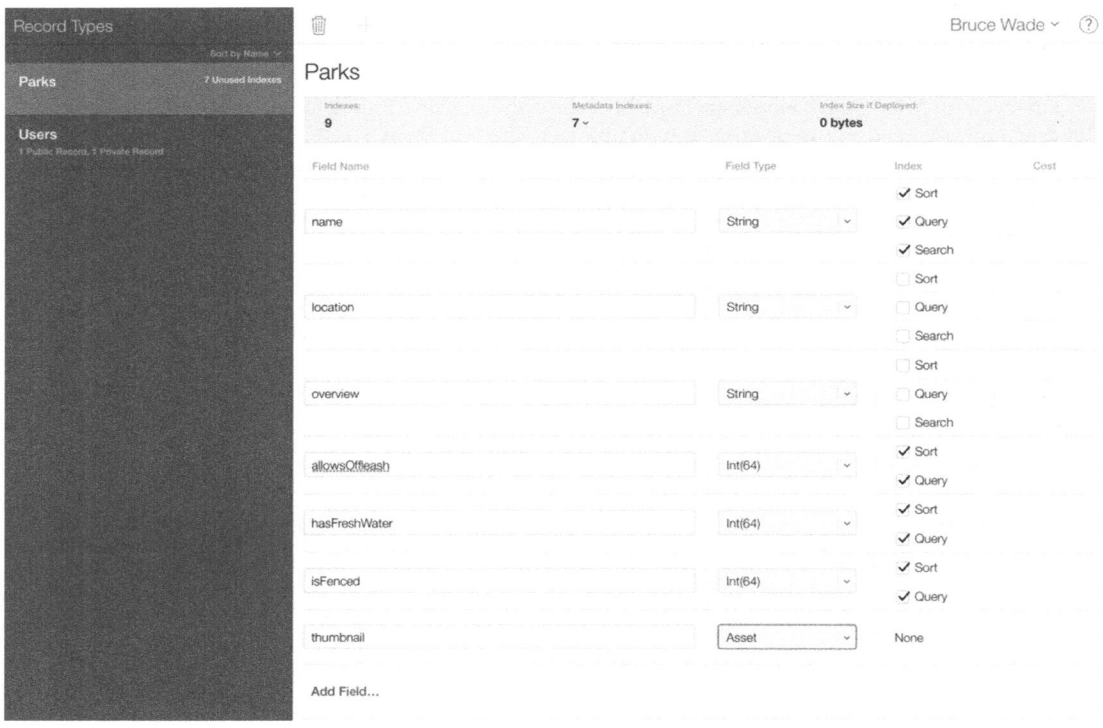

***Figure 5-2.*** *Complete Parks record type*

Next, we need to add the following fields to hold the data:

- name as a String with indexes for Sort, Query, and Search.
- location as a String (this can also use the Location type, which we might add later) with no indexes
- overview as String with no indexes
- allowsOffleash as an Int(64) with all the indexes
- hasFreshWater as an Int(64) with all the indexes
- isFenced as an Int(64) with all the indexes
- thumbnail as an Asset, which has no index options

We are using Int (64) for our Boolean fields because that is our only option with CloudKit; a value of 0 will mean the park doesn't have the feature and 1 will mean it does. Finally, click the Save button to save your changes. We will be using the thumbnail later as an optimization step.

# Creating the ParkImages Record Type

Now let's create another record type called Park Images. We will use this record type for each of our page images and use a back reference to the Park record they belong to. Create the type with the following fields (Figure 5-3):

- park as type Reference and index for Query. This will be used to link the parent park.
- thumbnail as an Asset type; this will be a smaller, scaled-down version of the main image used for optimization purposes
- image as an Asset type that will hold the full image

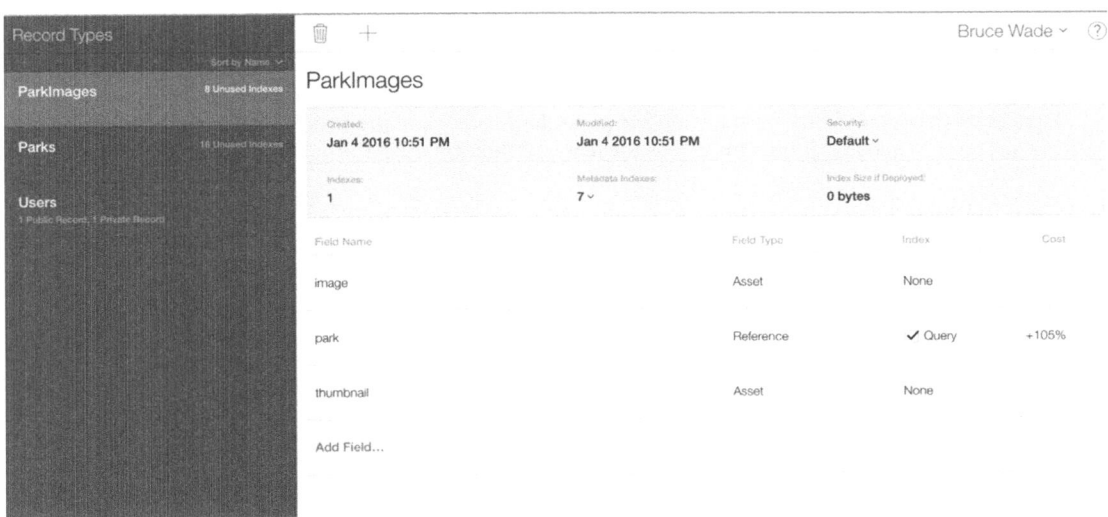

*Figure 5-3.* *Complete ParkImages record type*

# Security Role

Let's create a security role so only we can create a park. We will, however, allow others to add images to the park. Click on Security Roles, then create a ParkManager role, with a record type called Parks that has create, read, and write permissions. See Figure 5-4.

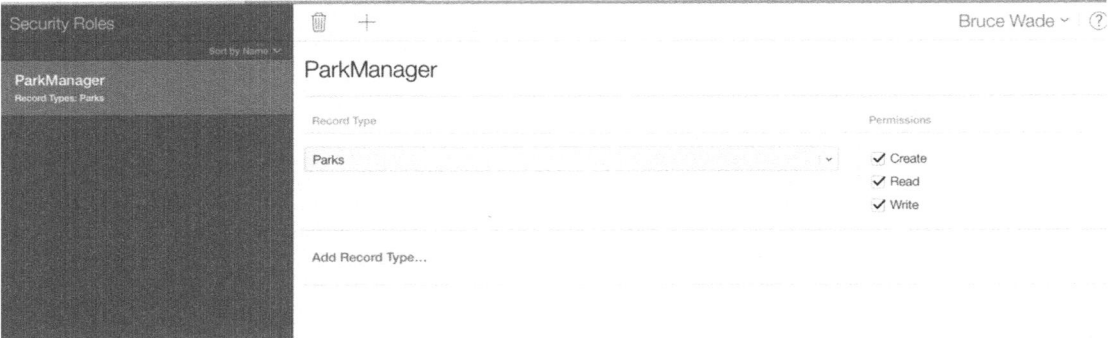

**Figure 5-4.** *ParkManager security role*

We will assign this role to our user at a later step once we integrate CloudKit into our app, as we currently have no users to assign the role to.

# Create Parks Test Data

Now that we have our record Types set up, we are going to create some sample data. I recommend that you search for parks in your area using Google; otherwise, local-based searching within the app won't work as expected. This will also get you into the habit of using real data and force you to think about what kind of data will be entered into the app.

We will create all of our test data in the Default Zone under public data. From the drop-down in the middle column, select "Parks." We'll start by creating some parks and then add images to the individual park.

First, enter the details from the following five parks. Either drag and drop your image into the Thumbnail field or click on the Upload button. This will be the featured thumbnail for the park in the Parks List.

```
1. name: Panorama Park
    allowsOffleash: 1
    hasFreshWater: 1
    isFenced: 0
    location: North Vancouver
    overview: Located in deep cove area.
    thumbnail: thumbnail.jpg (located in the TestParksData folder)
2. name: Kings Mill Park
    allowsOffleash: 1
    hasFreshWater: 1
    isFenced: 0
    location: North Vancouver
     overview: Good relaxing park to take your dogs to play.
     thumbnail: thumbnail.jpg (located in the TestParksData folder)
```

3. name: Deep Cove Park
   allowsOffleash: 0
   hasFreshWater: 0
   isFenced: 0
   location: North Vancouver
   overview: This park is located in the beautiful deep cove area.
   thumbnail: thumbnail.jpg (located in the TestParksData folder)
4. name: Bridgeman Park
   allowsOffleash: 1
   hasFreshWater: 1
   isFenced: 0
   location: North Vancouver
   overview: Provides a large park and walking trails where your dog can run around
   offleash. There is a stream with fresh moving water dogs can drink out of.
   thumbnail: thumbnail.jpg (located in the TestParksData folder)
5. name: Ambleside Dog Park
   allowsOffleash: 1
   hasFreshWater: 1
   isFenced: 0
   location: West Vancouver
   overview: Located off the ocean of Ambleside beach in West Vancouver.
   thumbnail: thumbnail.jpg (located in the TestParksData folder)

Click Save after each entry and your test park will be created (Figure 5-5). Repeat the process to create the other parks.

---

■ **Note**    You should scale the featured thumbnail to 48 x 48 to optimize bandwidth.

---

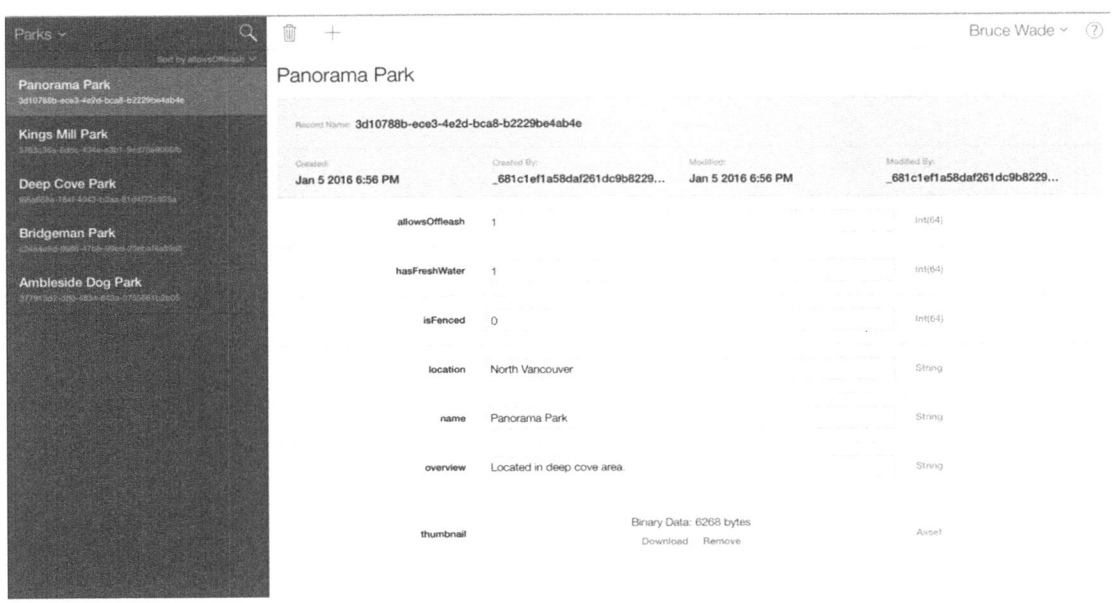

***Figure 5-5.*** *Sample park populated*

79

# Create ParkImages Test Data

For each park image contained within a park entry, you are also going to want to make a 90 x 90 pixel thumbnail version. Creating the thumbnails is an optimization, as there is no reason to download the full-size images if the user is only scrolling through a bunch of small images.

For each image you add to a park, you must provide the park's record name. You can find this by first finding the park you want to add an image to in the default data and copying its record name (Figure 5-6). Next, click the checkbox for "DeleteSelf," which will ensure that if the park record is deleted all images related to it will also be deleted.

*Figure 5-6.  Selected record name*

Next, change the middle column's drop-down selection to "ParkImages" and click the + to create a new record. You want to first focus on the Park field that is a Reference type. Paste the park record name you copied into the Park field textbox. At this point you will notice that all images show as No Name. (Figure 5-7). You can either leave it or add a Name field to the ParkImages record type and use it to name your images. For this book we will leave it as it is, though we may change this later.

*Figure 5-7.  ParkImages record type with a Parks record type name as a reference*

If you are following along using the test data provided with the book, within the Images folder for each park you will see a file following the naming convention of parkname#, and for the thumbnail that name is appended with 90x90. Drag the image without the 90x90 to the Image field, and drag the matching thumbnail to the Thumbnail field. Make sure to add multiple images for each park before moving on to the next chapter.

# Conclusion

This chapter has covered how the CloudKit Dashboard makes it very easy to create test data for your app. In the next chapter, we will upgrade our app so as to display this test data.

# CHAPTER 6

■ ■ ■

# Refining Our Prototype

In this chapter we will load the test data we created in CloudKit into our app. The app will show the list of parks, and when a user clicks on a park the app will display the park information inside the details plane.

## Creating the Park Model

With CloudKit being only a transport layer, we need a way to store and work with our information on the OS X client app. We need to create a simple Swift class Park that will store the information for an individual park. We will use the Swift class in a Swift list to store a list of parks. Create a new Swift file, name it Park, and update its contents as shown in Listing 6-1.

***Listing 6-1.*** Park Model Class

```
import Cocoa
import CloudKit

class Park: NSObject {
    var recordID: CKRecordID
    var name: String
    var overview: String
    var location: String
    var isFenced: Bool
    var hasFreshWater: Bool
    var allowsOffleash: Bool
    var thumbnail: NSImage?

    init(recordID: CKRecordID, name: String, overview: String, location: String, isFenced:
    Bool, hasFreshWater: Bool, allowsOffleash: Bool, thumbnailUrl: NSURL?) {

self.recordID = recordID
        self.name = name
        self.overview = overview
        self.location = location
        self.isFenced = isFenced
        self.hasFreshWater = hasFreshWater
        self.allowsOffleash = allowsOffleash
```

© Bruce Wade 2016

B. Wade, *OS X App Development with CloudKit and Swift*, DOI 10.1007/978-1-4842-1880-8_6

```
        if thumbnailUrl == nil {
            self.thumbnail = NSImage(named: "DefaultParkIcon")!
        } else {
            // TODO: Download image
        }


    }
}
```

We created a class Park that inherits from NSObject and contains the same properties we defined in CloudKit for our Parks record type, with the exception of the thumbnail, which is an NSImage type instead of an Asset type. For the thumbnail, we are going to include a default image sized to 48 x 48 pixels that will be used when a park does not have a thumbnail image provided. Everything else in this class is straightforward properties and an initializer. We are using a CKRecordID to enable us to query for the park images and also to make any updates we need to a park in a later chapter.

# CloudKit API

Ideally, when working with a backend web service such as CloudKit you want to abstract it away from the client, which will enable you to completely replace the backend service–say, from CloudKit to a custom Django API. It also enables you to use both CloudKit and an additional API without having to update any other part of the app.

Create a new Swift file named API; all of your CloudKit interaction will take place inside this file. Add imports for CloudKit and Cocoa to the top of the file. Then create a class called API that has no parent. Next, create two properties, one a constant to store the publicDB and the other an array to store our parks.

```
let publicDB = CKContainer.defaultContainer().publicCloudDatabase

var parks: [Park] = []
```

Now create a function to get a list of parks from CloudKit. Enter the code from Listing 6-2 inside your API class.

***Listing 6-2.*** Fetching the List of Parks

```
func fetchParks(completionHandler: [Park] -> Void) {
    let parksPredicate = NSPredicate(value: true)
    let query = CKQuery(recordType: "Parks", predicate: parksPredicate)

    publicDB.performQuery(query, inZoneWithID: nil) { [unowned self] (results, error) ->
Void in
        if error != nil {
            print("Error: \(error)")
        } else {
            for result in results! {
                let park = Park(
                    recordID: result["recordID"] as! CKRecordID,
                    name: result["name"] as! String,
                    overview: result["overview"] as! String,
                    location: result["location"] as! String,
                    isFenced: result["isFenced"] as! Bool,
```

```
                hasFreshWater: result["hasFreshWater"] as! Bool,
                allowsOffleash: result["allowsOffleash"] as! Bool,
                thumbnailUrl: nil
            )
            self.parks.append(park)
        }
        completionHandler(self.parks)
    }
  }
}
```

Our function takes in a closure that accepts an array of `Park` objects and returns nothing. We are using this `completionHandler` to pass back the list of parks to our calling code. We need this, because a query to CloudKit is asynchronous and so we don't know when we will get results returned.

We are using a predicate with a value of `true`, which simply means it will return all the results. This predicate could be updated to instead perform a geolocation search. Next, create a `CKQuery` telling it you want to query the Parks record type using the predicate just created. Finally, use the `publicDB` to perform the query, using the query you just created as a parameter. Since we are using the Default Zone, pass `nil` as the `inZoneWithID` parameter. This query will return us a closure that contains either a list of parks or an error. We are also using `[unowned self]` to ensure there are no circular references when we use the `Parks` array.

You should always check for errors by testing any error that occurs for a non-`nil` value. Here you can use the errors info dictionary to determine what error has occurred. If there are no errors you can loop over the results, creating a new `Park` object for each object returned. You create a new `Park` instance with the values that were returned from CloudKit, and then you append the new park to the `Parks` array. Finally, when the `for in` loop is finished, call the `completionHandler` passing in our `Parks` array. We have left the thumbnail as `nil` for the moment, as it requires additional code changes that we will address later.

That's it for the API for now. We will be updating it with more methods later.

# Populating ParkListViewController

Let's move over to our `ParkListViewController` and put our API to the test. We need to create two new properties, one a constant for the API and the other a variable for a dynamic array of `Park` objects.

```
let api = API()
dynamic var parks: [Park] = []
```

We initialize the API class so we can use it right away in code. It is best practice to have your API classes as singletons, so we will update our API class in a little while.

At the end of the `viewDidLoad` function, we add the call in Listing 6-3 to `fetchParks`.

***Listing 6-3.*** API Call to Get the List of Parks

```
api.fetchParks { [unowned self] (parks) -> Void in
    dispatch_async(dispatch_get_main_queue()) {
        self.parks = parks
    }
}
```

We have to use `dispatch_async` to update our local parks variable on the main queue because we are going to use data bindings to populate our interface.

# Setting Up Bindings

We are now going to set up bindings that will use our Parks array to populate the Table View with parks pulled from CloudKit.

Open Main.storyboard, then select the Table View inside the Document Outliner. Then, open the Bindings Inspector, and under Table Content check the "Bind to" checkbox and ensure "Park List View Controller" is selected. Finally, set the Model Key Path to self.parks (Figure 6-1).

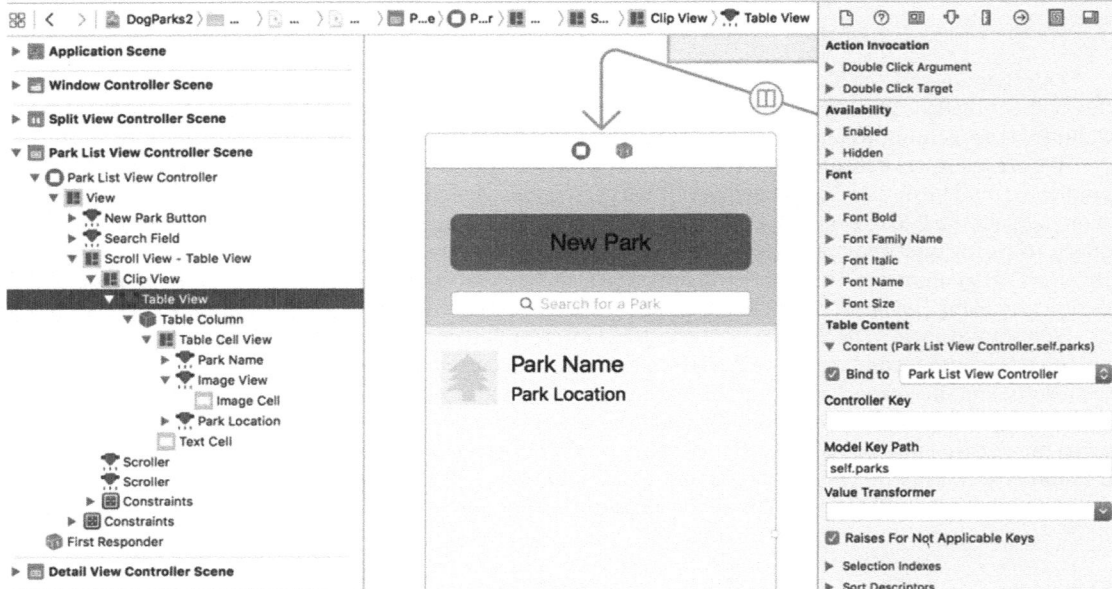

***Figure 6-1.*** *Selected Table View*

In the Document Outliner, select Park Name under Table Cell View. Then, in the Bindings Inspector under Value, check "Bind to" and select "Table Cell View." Now set the Model Key Path field to objectValue. name (Figure 6-2).

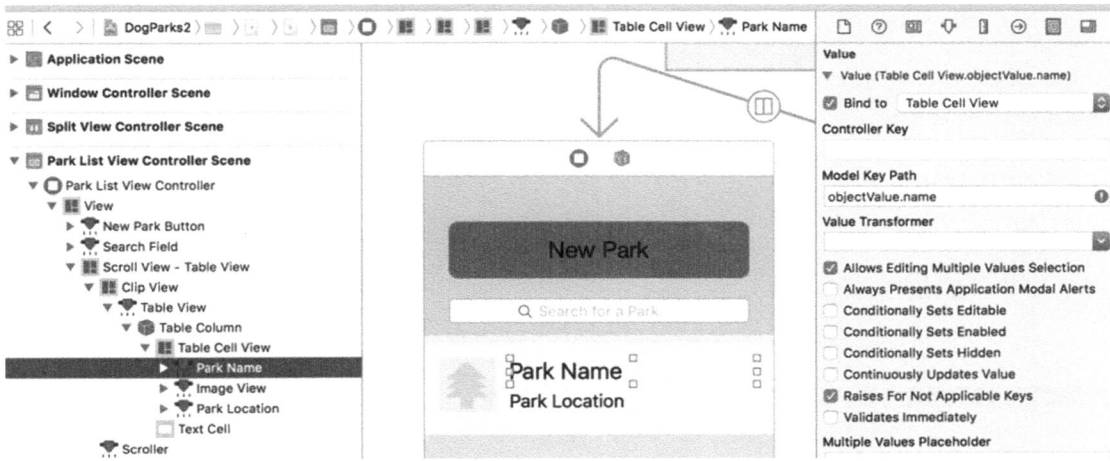

*Figure 6-2. Park name selection and data binding*

In the Document Outliner, select Image View under Table Cell View, then in the Bindings Inspector under Value check "Bind to" and select "Table Cell View." Now set the Model Key Path to objectValue. thumbnail (Figure 6-3).

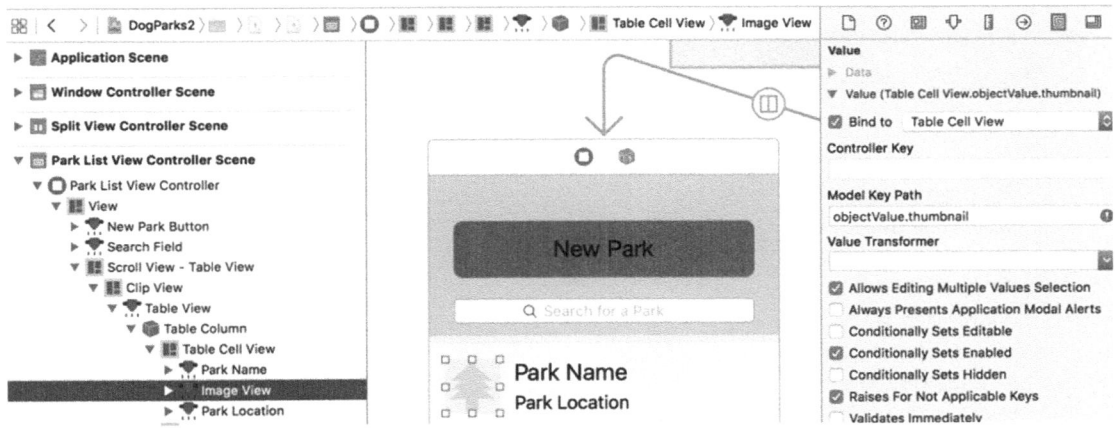

*Figure 6-3. Image View selected and data binding*

In the Document Outliner, select Park Location under Table Cell View, then in the Bindings Inspector under Value check "Bind to" and select "Table Cell View." Now set the Model Key Path to objectValue. location (Figure 6-4).

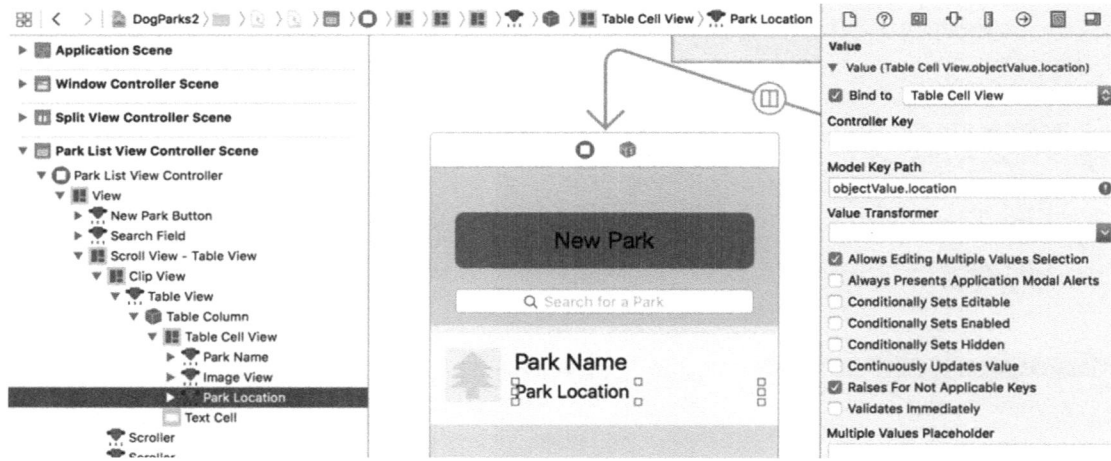

**Figure 6-4.** *Park Location selected and data bindings*

If you run the app now you should see the parks you created in the CloudKit Dashboard. The images you added still will not be displayed, and we will correct that next. Your app should now look like Figure 6-5.

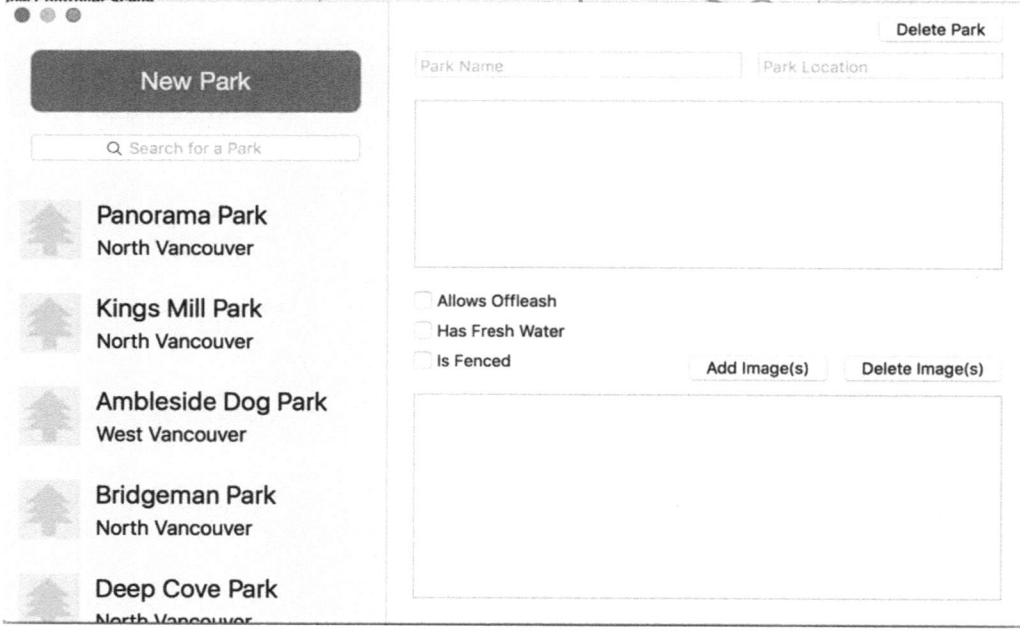

**Figure 6-5.** *Running app with populated parks from CloudKit*

# Downloading the Thumbnail Asset

Let's update our code so as to download the thumbnail assets from CloudKit. Inside the API Swift file, at the beginning of the for loop, add the code in Listing 6-4.

***Listing 6-4.*** Get the Image fileURL from a CKAsset

```
var thumbnailUrl: NSURL? = nil
if let thumbnail = result["thumbnail"] as? CKAsset {
    thumbnailUrl = thumbnail.fileURL
}
```

This code first creates an optional nil variable to hold the URL of the thumbnail. If there is no thumbnail asset for the target park, the default image will be used. We next check for a thumbnail asset. If one exists we get the fileURL. Next, we need to replace nil with the thumbnail when creating the park, so we use the new thumbnailUrl variable. Listing 6-5 shows the updated for in loop:

***Listing 6-5.*** Building the Park Objects from the Data Returned from CloudKit

```
for result in results! {
    var thumbnailUrl: NSURL? = nil
    if let thumbnail = result["thumbnail"] as? CKAsset {
        thumbnailUrl = thumbnail.fileURL
    }
    let park = Park(
        recordID: result["recordID"] as! CKRecordID,
        name: result["name"] as! String,
        overview: result["overview"] as! String,
        location: result["location"] as! String,
        isFenced: result["isFenced"] as! Bool,
        hasFreshWater: result["hasFreshWater"] as! Bool,
        allowsOffleash: result["allowsOffleash"] as! Bool,
        thumbnailUrl: thumbnailUrl
    )
    self.parks.append(park)
}
```

Now let's open the Park Swift file and replace the TODO comment with code to either download the thumbnail image if there is one or assign the default image if not. Replace the TODO comment with Listing 6-6.

***Listing 6-6.*** Set the Thumbnail on a Background Queue

```
dispatch_async(dispatch_get_global_queue(DISPATCH_QUEUE_PRIORITY_BACKGROUND, 0)) {
    if let imageData = NSData(contentsOfFile: (thumbnailUrl?.path)!) {
        self.thumbnail = NSImage(data: imageData)!
    }
}
```

Here, we are downloading the image to the background queue if we have a valid thumbnail URL. We use the path to create an NSData object, which we then use to set/download our thumbnail for the park.

# Handling Selecting a Park in the List

Let's now add an @IBAction that will be used to update the detail pane with information about the selected park.

Open ParkListViewController and add the function in Listing 6-7 after the awakeFromNib function.

*Listing 6-7.* Stub Action for Selecting a Park

```
@IBAction func selectPark(sender: AnyObject) {
    print("Selected park")
}
```

Now let's open Main.storyboard to connect the action. In the Document Outliner click the Table View within the Park List View Controller, and in the popup choose selectPark. Run the App; you should see "Selected Park" printed in the console when you click on a park (Figure 6-6).

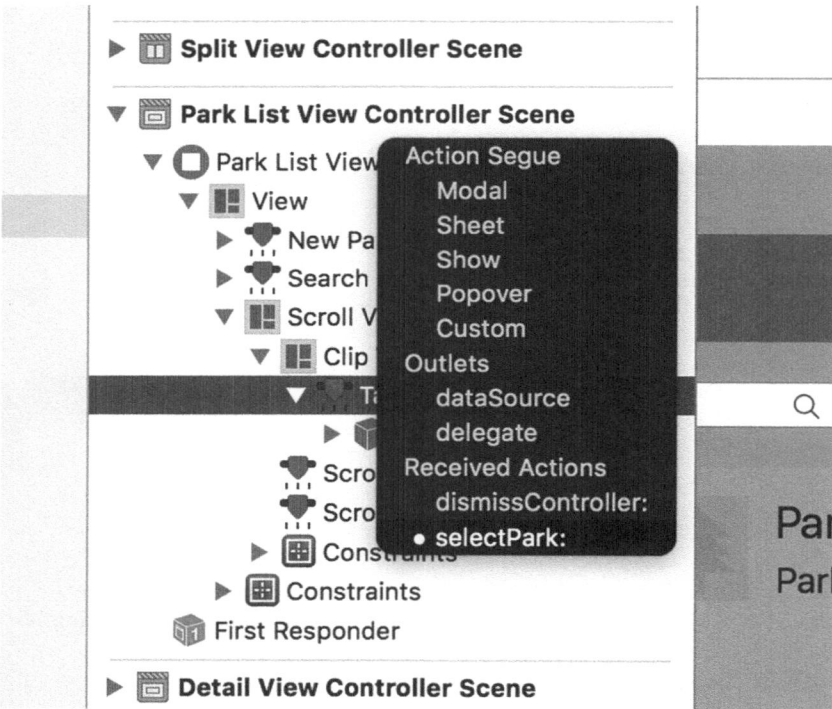

*Figure 6-6.* Connecting the "select park" action

In order to pass the selected park to the detail view controller, we are going to need to create a custom split view controller class, as well as a protocol that will be used by our custom controller to pass the park to our detail view controller.

Insert the protocol in Listing 6-8 at the top of the ParkListViewController file.

***Listing 6-8.*** Protocol for Handling Selected Parks

```
protocol ParkListViewControllerDelegate: class {
    func parkListViewController(viewController: ParkListViewController, selectedPark: Park?)
-> Void
}
```

Now create a new weak variable in the `ParkListViewController` for our delegate. We will use this delegate inside the `selectPark` action.

```
weak var delegate: ParkListViewControllerDelegate? = nil
```

Create a new Cocoa class with a subclass of `NSSplitViewController` and a name of `MainSplitViewController` (Figure 6-7).

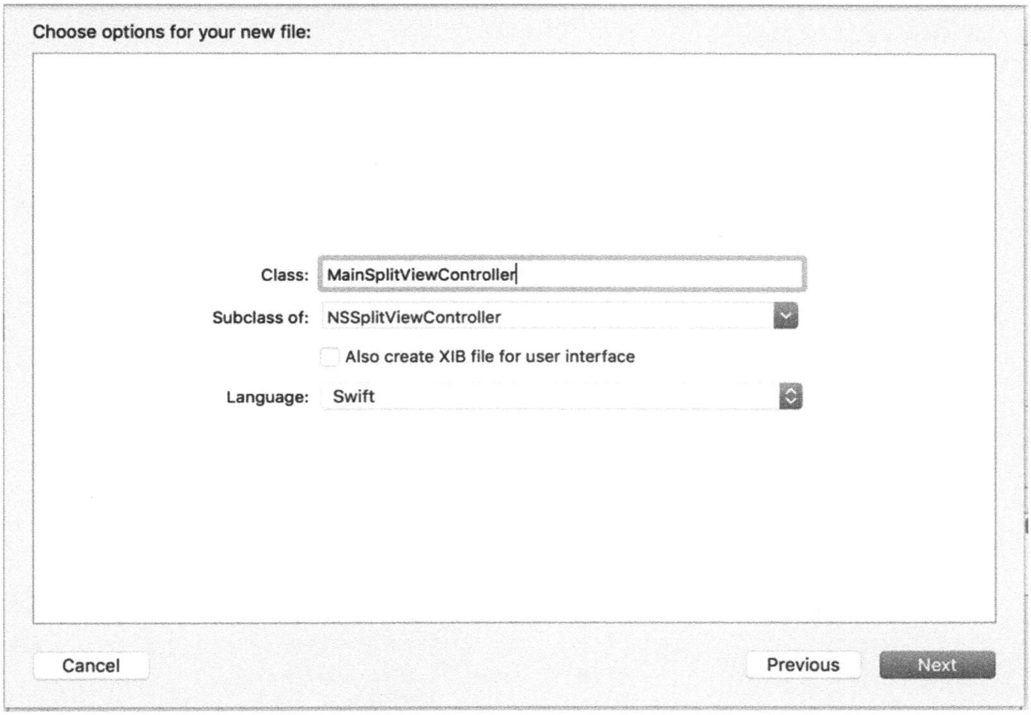

```
Choose options for your new file:



                        Class:  MainSplitViewController

                  Subclass of:  NSSplitViewController              ˅

                                  Also create XIB file for user interface

                     Language:  Swift                              ⌄



    Cancel                                        Previous        Next
```

***Figure 6-7.*** *Creating the MainSplitViewController class*

We are going to create two computed properties that will give us easy access to each of our view controllers, and also we will set our delegate property we just created to our `MainSplitViewController` instance. Finally, we will implement our custom protocol and load the new park into the detail controller. (At this point there will be an error, but we will fix that next.)

Update the `MainSplitViewController` contents to match Listing 6-9.

***Listing 6-9.*** Initial MainSplitViewController Class

```
import Cocoa

class MainSplitViewController: NSSplitViewController {

    var masterViewController: ParkListViewController {
        let masterItem = splitViewItems[0]
        return masterItem.viewController as! ParkListViewController
    }

    var detailViewController: DetailViewController {
        let masterItem = splitViewItems[1]
        return masterItem.viewController as! DetailViewController
    }

    override func viewDidLoad() {
        super.viewDidLoad()

        masterViewController.delegate = self
    }
}

extension MainSplitViewController: ParkListViewControllerDelegate {

    func parkListViewController(viewController: ParkListViewController, selectedPark: Park?) {
        detailViewController.loadPark(selectedPark)
    }
}
```

Before we fix the error, let's open the Main.storyboard and set the custom class for the SplitViewController to MainSplitViewController, as shown in Figure 6-8.

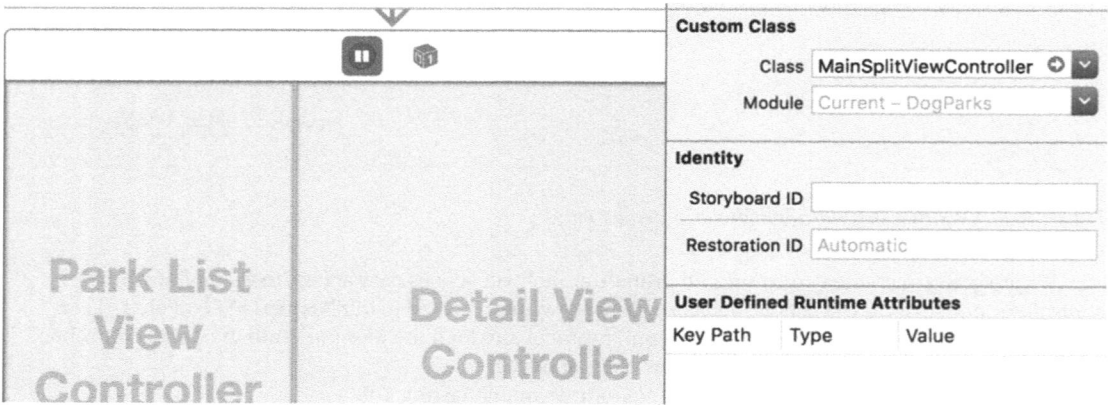

***Figure 6-8.*** *Setting up the split view controller to use our custom class*

Let's fix the error in our `MainSplitViewController`. Open the `DetailViewController` and add the following function to the `DetailViewController` class:

```
func loadPark(park: Park?) {
  print(park?.name)
}
```

In the `ParkListViewController` we are going to get the selected park and pass it through to our delegate, which in turn will pass it to our detail view controller.

Update the `selectPark` function to that seen in Listing 6-10.

*Listing 6-10.* Completed Action for Selecting a Park That Calls Our Delegate Method

```
@IBAction func selectPark(sender: AnyObject) {
    let selectedPark = parks[sender.selectedRow]
    delegate?.parkListViewController(self, selectedPark: selectedPark)
}
```

First, we get the `selectedRow` from the sender and use that as an index into our `Parks` array to get the correct park. Then, we pass the selected park to our delegate method, which is set to our `MainSplitViewController`.

If you run the app now and select a row, you will see that the park's name is printed in the console.

# Update DetailViewController

Now that we are passing the selected park to the detail view controller, it is time to populate our interface with the park's information.

First, let's create a private dynamic park variable and then update the `loadPark` function to update that variable. See Listing 6-11.

*Listing 6-11.* Assign the Selected Park to the Detail View Controller

```
private dynamic var park: Park? = nil
func loadPark(park: Park?) {
  self.park = park
}
```

Now we are going to use bindings to update the UI whenever the selected park changes. Select the Park Name textfield, and in the Bindings Inspector under Value, check "Bind to" and select "Detail View Controller," then set the Model Key Path to `self.park.name` (Figure 6-9).

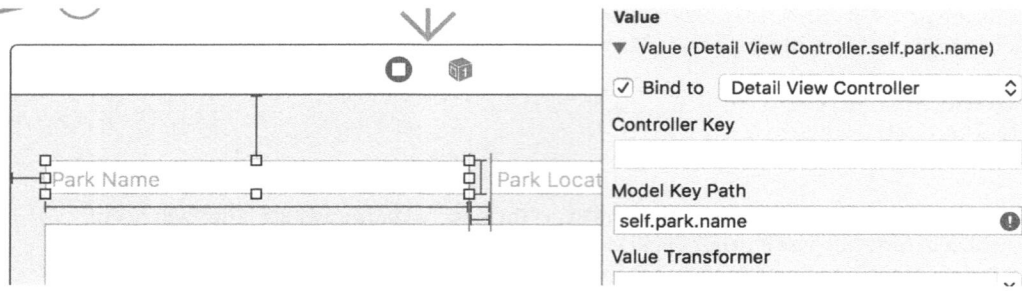

**Figure 6-9.** *Data-binding setup for the park name*

Repeat the same process for the Park Location field, changing the Model Key Path to `self.park.location`.

For the park overview, use the Document Outliner to select the Text View, and then set the binding for the Attributed String under Value to bind to "Detail View Controller," with the Model Key Path set to `self.park.overview` (Figure 6-10).

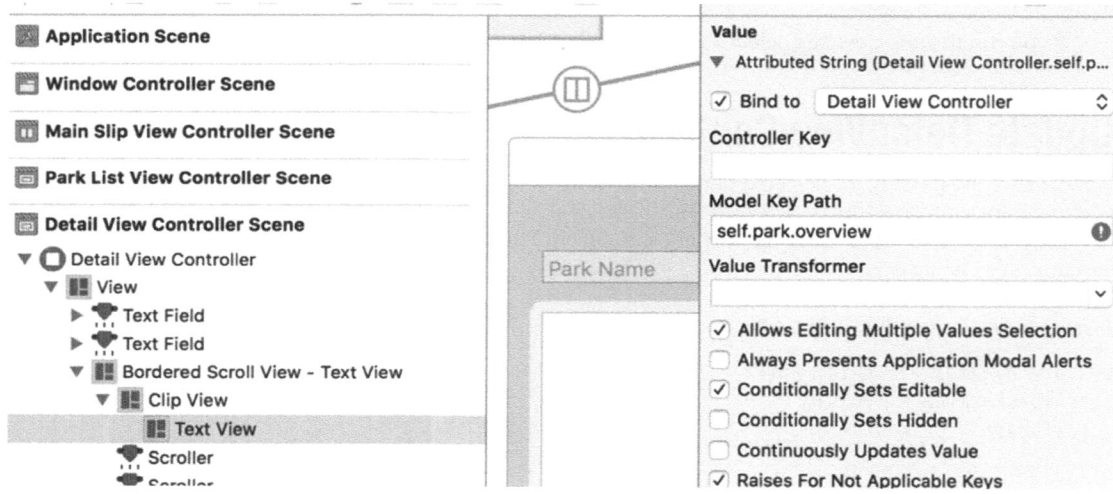

**Figure 6-10.** *Data binding for the park overview Text View*

# Downloading Park Images for the Selected Park

Our final tasks for this chapter are downloading any park images related to this park and then adding them to the `parkImagesCollection` of the specific park selected by the user.

First, we need to create a new class that will store our image data. Create a new Swift file called `ParkImage` and update its contents with the code in Listing 6-12.

*Listing 6-12.* Code for the ParkImage Class

```
import Cocoa
import CloudKit

class ParkImage: NSObject {
    var recordID: CKRecordID
    var thumbnail: NSImage?
    var imageURL: NSURL?

 var image: NSImage?

    init(recordID: CKRecordID, thumbnailUrl: NSURL?, imageURL: NSURL?) {
        self.recordID = recordID
        self.imageURL = imageURL

        super.init()

        if thumbnailUrl != nil {
            dispatch_async(dispatch_get_global_queue(DISPATCH_QUEUE_PRIORITY_
            BACKGROUND, 0)) {
                if let imageData = NSData(contentsOfFile: (thumbnailUrl?.path)!) {
                    self.thumbnail = NSImage(data: imageData)!
                }
            }
        }

    }
}
```

We are importing CloudKit only to use CKRecordID. I'm sure there are other ways to do this without relying on CKRecordID; however, we will just keep it simple. The fields are the same as we have in our ParkImages record type, with the addition of imageURL. There is no need to create the actual full-size image at this point, so we are just storing the path. We do, however, load the thumbnail if there is one inside the init method.

Next, let's update our API to handle fetching park images related to the selected park. Open API.swift and add the function from Listing 6-13.

*Listing 6-13.* Method to Select All the Related Park Images

```
func fetchParkImages(parkRecordID: CKRecordID, completionHandler: [ParkImage] -> Void) {
    let reference = CKReference(recordID: parkRecordID, action: CKReferenceAction.DeleteSelf)
    let pred = NSPredicate(format: "park == %@", reference)
    let sort = NSSortDescriptor(key: "creationDate", ascending: true)
    let query = CKQuery(recordType: "ParkImages", predicate: pred)
    query.sortDescriptors = [sort]

    parkImages = []
```

```
publicDB.performQuery(query, inZoneWithID: nil) { [unowned self] (results, error)
-> Void in
  if error != nil {
    print(error!.localizedDescription)
  } else {
    for result in results! {
        var thumbnailUrl: NSURL? = nil
        if let thumbnail = result["thumbnail"] as? CKAsset {
            thumbnailUrl = thumbnail.fileURL
        }
        var imageUrl: NSURL? = nil
        if let image = result["image"] as? CKAsset {
            imageUrl = image.fileURL
        }
        let parkImage = ParkImage(
            recordID: result["recordID"] as! CKRecordID,

thumbnailUrl: thumbnailUrl,
            imageURL: imageUrl
        )
        self.parkImages.append(parkImage)
        }
        completionHandler(self.parkImages)
    }
  }
}
```

This method takes in a park record ID, which it uses to create a reference that we will utilize to find all park images in the app related to this park. It also takes in a completionHandler that we use to pass back all the park images returned by the reference.

The first line creates a CKReference using the parkRecordID and tells it to delete the image if the parent park is deleted. This is only really important if we are creating a new park image; however, we are not at this point and are only using the reference to query.

Next, we create an NSPredicate that finds all the park images with a park reference that matches the one we just created. In other words, it says "find all park images that belong to this park."

Then, we create an NSSortDescriptor to order our images into ascending order based on the creationDate field. CreationDate is a field that is automatically created by CloudKit.

The next line ensures that our local parkImages array is empty. If we don't do this, every call to this API function will just keep appending new images for each park we click on, which isn't what we want.

We now have the information we require to create a CKQuery. We tell CKQuery we want to search the ParkImages record type using the NSPredicate we just created. Then, we assign our sort descriptor to the query.

Finally, we use the public database to perform the query, passing in the query we just created and a nil zone ID, as we are not using zones.

If there are no errors, we loop through the results, getting the image URLs as we did in the other API function. Then, we create a park image and add it to our local parkImages array. Once we are finished with the loop, we pass in the array of images to the completionHandler.

Now we need to update our detail view controller. First, create a new IBOutlet for an NSArrayController. We will use this to work with the content of our parkImagesCollection we created earlier:

```
@IBOutlet var imagesArrayController: NSArrayController!
```

Next, we need to create a constant for our API, as well as another private dynamic variable to store our park images:

```
let api = API()
private dynamic var parkImages: [ParkImage] = []
```

Now we need to update our loadPark function to handle fetching and updating the imagesArrayController, which in turn will update the parkImagesCollection. Update the loadPark function to look like Listing 6-14.

***Listing 6-14.*** Updated Load Park Method to Handle Fetching Park Images

```
func loadPark(park: Park?) {
    self.park = park

    parkImages = []

    if self.park != nil {
        api.fetchParkImages((self.park?.recordID)!, completionHandler: { [unowned self]
        (parkImages) -> Void in
            if parkImages.count > 0 {
                dispatch_async(dispatch_get_main_queue()) {
                            self.imagesArrayController.addObjects(parkImages)

                }
            }
        })
    }
}
```

In the first new line we ensure the reset of the parkImages array. Next, we make sure there is an existing park. Then, we call our new API method, passing in our park recordID. Finally, we check to make sure there were some images returned, and if there were we call addObjects on the array controller. This method allows us to add multiple images at once instead of looping over all the returned images and adding them one by one.

Lastly, we must update our storyboard to connect everything together. Open the Main.storyboard file. In the Object Library find the array Controller. We need to drag this onto the detail view controller. Figure 6-11 shows the array controller in object list. The top of the detail view controller shows an array controller has been attached.

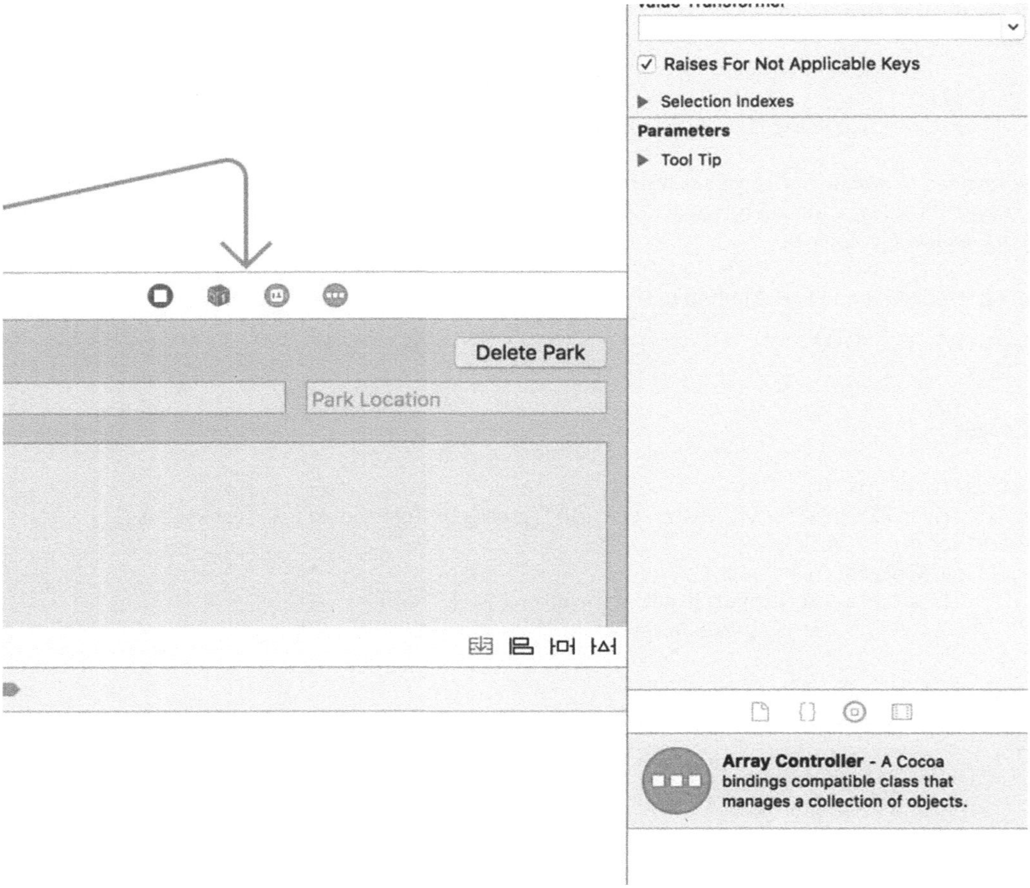

**Figure 6-11.** *Array controller attached in object list*

In the Document Outliner, press Control and drag from the Detail View Controller down to the Array Controller, and in the Outlets popup select the option for imagesArrayController (Figure 6-12).

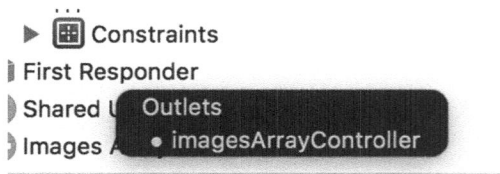

**Figure 6-12.** *Connecting the imagesArrayController outlet to the new array controller*

Still in the Document Outliner, find the Park Images Collection. In the Bindings Inspector under Content, check "Bind to" and select "Images Array Controller," with the Controller Key set to arrangedObjects (Figure 6-13). If you forget this binding, the array controller and the collection will not be connected, meaning no images will show up.

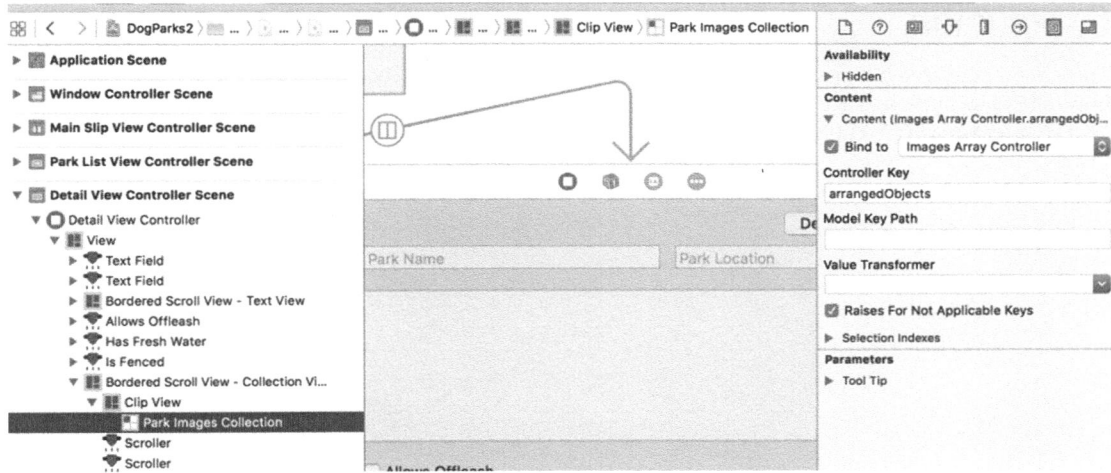

**Figure 6-13.** *Park images collection binding to the images array controller*

In the Collection View item, select the Image View, and under Value check "Bind to" and select "Collection View Item." Set Model Key Path to `representedObject.thumbnail`.

Finally, select the Images Array Controller and update its binding for the controller content to bind to the detail view controller with a model key path of `self.parkImages`.

Now if you run the app and select a park with images, everything should work as expected (Figure 6-14).

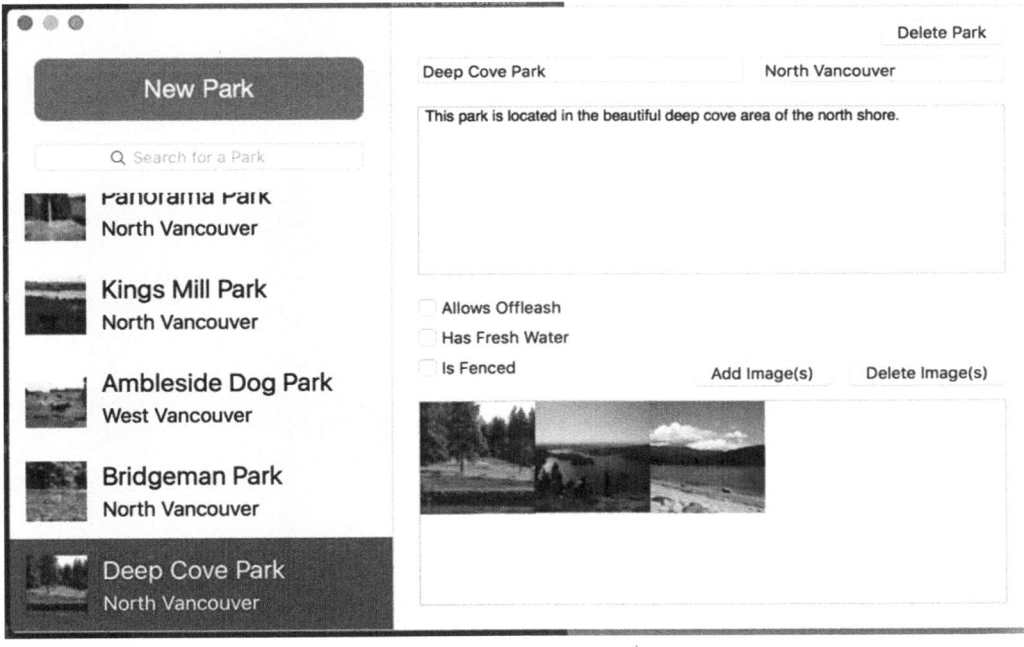

**Figure 6-14.** *Running app with a selected park and its data displayed in the detail view controller*

# Conclusion

This chapter covered taking our app, which had no data, and having it load data from CloudKit. We covered how to load all parks or a selected park, and how to then query and load references for a selected park. In the next chapter we will cover how to update the data we pulled from CloudKit from inside our app.

# CHAPTER 7

# Updating CloudKit Data from Our App

In the last chapter we got our app working with dynamic data pulled from the CloudKit servers. In this chapter we will update our app to allow us to change existing CloudKit data, create new data for our record types, and finally to delete data from CloudKit servers.

## Updating Existing Data

Let's take a look at how to update a park when it is changed within our app. First, we need to update our API with a helper method to prevent code duplication. This helper method's job is to convert the park CKRecord into a Park object. Copy the code inside the fetchParks for-in statement up to but not including the line that adds the new park to the array. With that code, create the new function in Listing 7-1.

*Listing 7-1.* Code to Convert CKRecord to a Park Object

```
private func convertCKRecordToPark(parkRecord: CKRecord) -> Park {
    var thumbnailUrl: NSURL? = nil
    if let thumbnail = parkRecord["thumbnail"] as? CKAsset {
        thumbnailUrl = thumbnail.fileURL
    }
    let savedPark = Park(
        recordID: parkRecord["recordID"] as! CKRecordID,
        name: parkRecord["name"] as? String ?? "",
        overview: parkRecord["overview"] as? String ?? "",
        location: parkRecord["location"] as? String ?? "",
        isFenced: parkRecord["isFenced"] as? Bool ?? false,

hasFreshWater: parkRecord["hasFreshWater"] as? Bool ?? false,
        allowsOffleash: parkRecord["allowsOffleash"] as? Bool ?? false,
        thumbnailUrl: thumbnailUrl)
    return savedPark
}
```

Now replace the code you just copied with a call to the method in the `fetchParks` function (Listing 7-2).

*Listing 7-2.* Updated for-loop to Use Our New Convert Method

```
for result in results! {
    let park = self.convertCKRecordToPark(result)
    self.parks.append(park)
}
```

With that in place, let's create a new function that will update our park. We are going to take advantage of the CloudKit convenience API, which requires us to first fetch our park record from the server, then update the fetched record, and finally save it back to the server. Add the following function to our `API.swift` file (Listing 7-3).

*Listing 7-3.* Updating and Saving the Park to CloudKit Using Our New Convert Method

```
func updatePark(park: Park, completionHandler: Park -> Void) {

    // Get any changes for the park from the server
    publicDB.fetchRecordWithID(park.recordID) { (parkRecord, error) -> Void in
        if error != nil {
            print(error!.localizedDescription)
        } else {
            // Currently just overriding as we are the only ones using this app.
            parkRecord!["name"] = park.name
            parkRecord!["location"] = park.location
            parkRecord!["overview"] = park.overview
            parkRecord!["isFenced"] = park.isFenced
            parkRecord!["hasFreshWater"] = park.hasFreshWater
            parkRecord!["allowsOffleash"] = park.allowsOffleash

            // Save update back to the server
            self.publicDB.saveRecord(parkRecord!, completionHandler: { (parkRecord, error) ->
            Void in
                if error != nil {
                    print(error!.localizedDescription)
                } else {
                    completionHandler(self.convertCKRecordToPark(parkRecord!))
                }
            })
        }
    }
}
```

This method first queries the CloudKit servers using the park `recordID`, then if there are no errors the returned record is updated with the new park data from our app, and finally we save the record back to the server. If there are no errors we pass the `completionHandler` a call to our helper method, which will convert the `CKRecord` into a `Park` object our app can use.

Now let's open the `DetailViewController` and create a new `IBAction` that will save the record for us. There are also other ways to handle this that save the record whenever the bound park changes; however, that is out of the scope of this book.

Add an action to the bottom of the detail view controller (Listing 7-4).

***Listing 7-4.*** Code That Uses the API to Save a Park

```
@IBAction func savePark(sender: AnyObject) {

    if let park = self.park {
        api.updatePark(park) { [unowned self] (updatedPark) -> Void in
            dispatch_async(dispatch_get_main_queue()) {
                self.park = updatedPark
            }
        }
    }
}
```

Next, let's open the storyboard, where we need to create a new button for saving the record and also connect it to our action. Drag a button next to the Delete Park button and set its title to Save Park. Pin it to the right and top. Finally, press Control and drag from the Save Park button to the detail view controller icon (blue with a white square); in the popup under Received Actions choose savePark (Figure 7-1).

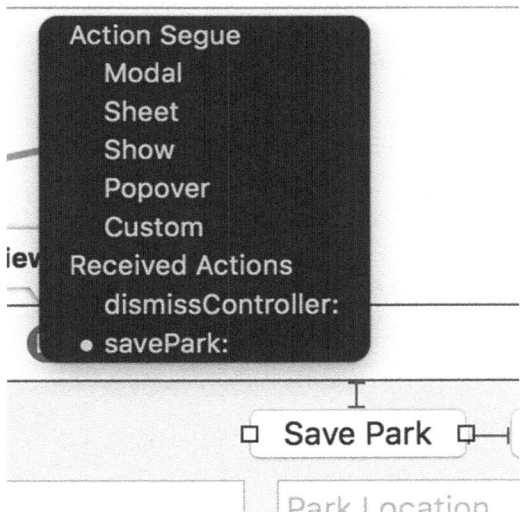

***Figure 7-1.*** *Save Park button connected to the savePark action*

Now if you run the app you will see an error about write permissions. This is where our custom permissions we created earlier come into play. We could have allowed anyone to update records; however, we are going to limit it to people with the correct permissions. Go back to the CloudKit Dashboard and under Public Data chose User Records, then select your user record. Set the security roles to ParkManager and save the record. If you run the app again you should have no issues saving. It is important to note that if you update a text field you will have to click outside of it before clicking Save if you also want the park list to update. Make some changes and save the park, then stop the app and start it again to make sure your park is updated.

# Creating New Data

We need to create two different types of objects in our app: parks and park images for each park. First, we need to update our API to handle creating new parks. Create a new function in your API.swift file (Listing 7-5).

***Listing 7-5.*** New API Method to Handle Saving a New Park Record

```
func createPark(completionHandler: Park -> Void) {
    let newParkRecord = CKRecord(recordType: "Parks")
    newParkRecord["name"] = "New Park"

    publicDB.saveRecord(newParkRecord) { (newPark, error) -> Void in
      if error != nil {
        print(error!.localizedDescription)
      } else {
            completionHandler(self.convertCKRecordToPark(newPark!))
      }
    }
}
```

In this function we simply create a new CKRecord of type Parks, set the name property to New Park, then use the convenience API to save the record. If everything saves as expected, we call our completion handler and pass it the New Park object.

In ParkListViewController we need to make two updates. First, we need an IBOutlet for accessing our Table View, and second, we need a new IBAction for creating new parks. Add the IBOutlet under the newParkButton outlet.

```
@IBOutlet weak var tableView: NSTableView!
```

Next, at the end of the controller class, add a new action with the code in Listing 7-6.

***Listing 7-6.*** New Action That Uses Our API to Save a Park

```
@IBAction func createPark(sender: AnyObject) {
    api.createPark { [unowned self] (newPark) -> Void in
      dispatch_async(dispatch_get_main_queue()) {
        self.parks.append(newPark)
            self.tableView.selectRowIndexes(NSIndexSet(index: self.parks.endIndex-1),
            byExtendingSelection: false)
            self.tableView.scrollRowToVisible(self.parks.endIndex-1)
        self.delegate?.parkListViewController(self, selectedPark: self.parks.last)
      }
    }
}
```

Inside this action we call our createPark API method, and then on the main queue we add the new park to our array. We next tell the Table View to select our new park and to delete anything that was already selected. Next, we tell the Table View to scroll down to our new park. Finally, we tell our detail view controller to use the data from our new park.

If you run the app you should now be able to create a new park. You can verify in the CloudKit Dashboard that the park is saved, and you can also update and save any changes.

Let's move on to adding park images before we look at how to delete objects from CloudKit.

We are first going to create an extension for NSImage that will enable us to create thumbnails and also save them to a file. Create a new Swift file named NSImageExtension and replace its contents with the code in Listing 7-7.

***Listing 7-7.*** Helper Code for Creating a Thumbnail

```
import Cocoa

extension NSImage {

    func makeThumbnail(width: CGFloat, _ height: CGFloat) -> NSImage {
        let thumbnail = NSImage(size: CGSizeMake(width, height))

        thumbnail.lockFocus()
        let context = NSGraphicsContext.currentContext()
        context?.imageInterpolation = .High
        self.drawInRect(NSMakeRect(0, 0, width, height), fromRect: NSMakeRect(0, 0,
        size.width, size.height), operation: .CompositeCopy, fraction: 1)
        thumbnail.unlockFocus()

        return thumbnail
    }

    func saveTo(filePath: String) {
        let bmpImageRep: NSBitmapImageRep = NSBitmapImageRep(data: TIFFRepresentation!)!
        addRepresentation(bmpImageRep)

        let data: NSData = bmpImageRep.representationUsingType(.NSJPEGFileType,
        properties: [:])!

        data.writeToFile(filePath, atomically: false)
    }
}
```

The first function, makeThumbnail, allows us to pass in a width and height that will be used to scale or crop an image to the specified size. The details of how exactly this function works are not in the scope of this book; just know that it returns a new thumbnail image that is the size you pass in using the data from the original image.

The second function, saveTo(filePath: String), takes in the complete file path of where we want to write the temporary thumbnail to on disk. We need to create an NSBitmapImageRep and add it to our current NSImage instance. We use this to create the NSData object that is finally used to write our file to disk.

With these helper methods in place, let's move over to our API.swift file. We will first create a new function for converting ParkImages record types into ParkImage objects like we did for Parks. At the bottom of the class add the code from Listing 7-8.

***Listing 7-8.*** Code to Convert a CKRecord into a ParkImage Object

```
private func convertCKRecordToParkImage(parkImageRecord: CKRecord) -> ParkImage {
    var thumbnailUrl: NSURL? = nil
    if let thumbnail = parkImageRecord["thumbnail"] as? CKAsset {
        thumbnailUrl = thumbnail.fileURL
    }
    var imageUrl: NSURL? = nil
    if let image = parkImageRecord["image"] as? CKAsset {
        imageUrl = image.fileURL
    }
    let parkImage = ParkImage(
        recordID: parkImageRecord["recordID"] as! CKRecordID,
        thumbnailUrl: thumbnailUrl,
        imageURL: imageUrl
    )
    return parkImage
}
```

There is nothing new here. This is the same code that was inside the for-in loop of the `fetchParkImages` API call. Replace the code in the `for-in` loop with the following:

```
self.parkImages.append(self.convertCKRecordToParkImage(result))
```

Now let's create a new API method that will be used to save the park images that are added to a given park. This method is going to need to know what park these images belong to, so we will provide it the `parkRecordID`. It will also need a list of `imageUrls`, as well as a `completionHandler` where we can pass all the images that were uploaded successfully.

This method is more complicated than the rest we have seen because we need to use `CKReferences`, and we also need to make thumbnails from a file that has been selected so that we can upload both the thumbnail and the original image. Finally, we are using `CKModifyRecordsOperation`, which will enable us to save multiple records at once. We are doing this because we want to allow the user to select multiple records, or images, at once instead of a single file at a time. Create the new function with the code in Listing 7-9.

***Listing 7-9.*** Saving Multiple Records to CloudKit at Once

```
func saveParkImages(parkRecordID: CKRecordID, imageUrls: [NSURL], completionHandler:
[ParkImage] -> Void) {

    var tempThumbnailFiles = [String]()
    var imageRecordsToUpload = [CKRecord]()

    for imageUrl in imageUrls {
        // Get file name
        let originalFileName = imageUrl.URLByDeletingPathExtension!.lastPathComponent!
        let thumbnailFileName = "/tmp/\(originalFileName)_90x90.jpg"
        tempThumbnailFiles.append(thumbnailFileName)

        // Create a thumbnail from the original image
        let originalImage = NSImage(contentsOfURL: imageUrl)
        let thumbnailImage = originalImage?.makeThumbnail(90, 90)
```

```
        // Save the thumbnail to a file
        thumbnailImage?.saveTo(thumbnailFileName)

        let record = CKRecord(recordType: "ParkImages")
        record["park"] = CKReference(recordID: parkRecordID, action: .DeleteSelf)
        record["image"] = CKAsset(fileURL: imageUrl)
        record["thumbnail"] = CKAsset(fileURL: NSURL(fileURLWithPath: thumbnailFileName))
        imageRecordsToUpload.append(record)
    }

    let uploadOperation = CKModifyRecordsOperation(recordsToSave: imageRecordsToUpload,
    recordIDsToDelete: nil)
    uploadOperation.atomic = false
    uploadOperation.database = publicDB

    uploadOperation.modifyRecordsCompletionBlock = { (savedRecords: [CKRecord]?,
    deletedRecords: [CKRecordID]?, operationError: NSError?) -> Void in
      guard operationError == nil else {
        print(operationError!.localizedDescription)
        return
      }
      if let records = savedRecords {
        var imagesUploaded = [ParkImage]()
        for parkImageRecord in records {
          // Create a new ParkImage record and append it to array of imagesUploaded
                imagesUploaded.append(self.convertCKRecordToParkImage(parkImageRecord))
        }

        // Now that we know our file was uploaded, delete temp local files.
        for tempThumbnailFile in tempThumbnailFiles {
          do {
            try NSFileManager.defaultManager().removeItemAtPath(tempThumbnailFile)
          } catch _ {
              print("Couldn't delete file: \(tempThumbnailFile)")
          }
        }

        completionHandler(imagesUploaded)
      }
    }

    NSOperationQueue().addOperation(uploadOperation)
}
```

We are creating temporary thumbnail files, so we need to make sure we clean up after ourselves. Therefore, we create a variable, tempThumbnailFiles, to store the complete file paths as we create them. We are also going to be creating multiple CKRecords, which will be saved all together instead of one by one, so we create an imageRecordsToUpload variable to store the array of CKRecords.

Next, we loop over the list of imageUrls. First, we get the file name without the path extension from the imageUrl. We then use that name and add _90x90.jpg to it so it's clear what image size we are creating, and then append it to the /tmp/ directory. We then append the full path to our thumbnailFiles array.

In the next step, we need to use the imageUrl to create an NSImage and then use *that* image to make a thumbnail. Finally, we save the thumbnail to the file path we just created.

In the final part of the loop, we create the CKRecord of ParkImages type. We use the parkRecordID we passed in to create a CKReference and set the action to .DeleteSelf, which means if the park is deleted this image and others linked to the park will be deleted as well. We use the imageUrl as a CKAsset for the full-size image, and the full path to the thumbnail we just created as the CKAsset for the thumbnail. We then add the record to our imageRecordsToUpload array that we will be using shortly.

Next, we create a CKModifyRecordsOperation and use it to pass our imageRecordsToUpload and nil as the records to delete. We tell the operation that we do not need every save to succeed. Finally, we tell the operation that we are using the public database; this is also the other reason atomic is set to false, as it is only supported in private record zones.

Now we must create a completion block that will be called when all the records have been saved. There is also another completion block that can be used for each record save; however, we are not using it here. This completion block is passed in the saved records, any deleted records, and any errors, if there were any.

We must first check if there were any errors, and if there were we print out the error and exit out of the completion block. If there were no errors we loop through the records returned and convert them to ParkImage objects, adding them to our imagesUploaded array.

Next, we will clean up all the temporary files we created when making the thumbnails. We do this using the NSFileManager and by looping through our tempThumbnailFiles array, deleting each file in the list.

At the end of the completion block we call our completionHandler, passing in our array of ParkImages.

Lastly, at the end of the function we add the operation we just created to the NSOperationQueue.

The last thing we need to do is create an action that will be used to allow users to upload images to the park pages. We will attach this action to our Add Image(s) button. We will be taking advantage of the standard NSOpenPanel to handle this for us. We tell the open panel to look for image files, that we can select multiple files (holding Shift or Command to select them), and that we can actually choose files. Finally, we call the beginWithCompletionHandler on the open panel to open the panel. This completion handler will provide us with a list of file URLs that we can pass to our API to upload. We also use our current park instance and pass the recordID to our API. See Listing 7-10.

***Listing 7-10.*** Selecting Images from the File System and Using Our API to Save Them to CloudKit

```
@IBAction func addImages(sender: AnyObject) {
    let openPanel = NSOpenPanel()
    openPanel.allowsMultipleSelection = true
    openPanel.canChooseDirectories = false
    openPanel.canCreateDirectories = false
    openPanel.canChooseFiles = true
    openPanel.allowedFileTypes = NSImage.imageUnfilteredTypes()
    openPanel.beginWithCompletionHandler { (result) -> Void in

      if result == NSFileHandlingPanelOKButton {
        self.api.saveParkImages((self.park?.recordID)!, imageUrls: openPanel.URLs,
        completionHandler: { (parkImages) -> Void in
          dispatch_async(dispatch_get_main_queue()) {
                    self.imagesArrayController.addObjects(parkImages)
          }
        })
      }
    }
}
```

Now open the Main.storyboard and Control-drag from the Add Image(s) button to the detail view controller; in the popup select addImages. Run the app now and you should be able to add multiple images to a park. (Note there is a short delay, as currently we are uploading the images then downloading them again before we update the collection view).

# Deleting a Park

In this section we are going to look at deleting an entire park, which will also delete any images related to it. Then we will look at how we can delete a park image(s).

Let's update our API to support deleting parks. Open API.swift and add the code seen in Listing 7-11.

*Listing 7-11.* API Method to Handle Deleting a Park

```
func deletePark(parkRecordID: CKRecordID, completionHandler: NSError? -> Void) {
    publicDB.deleteRecordWithID(parkRecordID) { (deletedRecordID, error) -> Void in
        completionHandler(error)
    }
}
```

Here we use the deleteRecordWithID method from the CloudKit convenience API. We pass the record ID for the park and a completionHandler call into our deletePark method. We then pass the completionHandler the error, if there is one.

Now we need to make changes in a few different places. We will first update our ParkListViewControllerDelegate to the following. Notice we have removed the view controller parameter because we determined we don't need it. Open ParkListViewController and update the delegate to look like Listing 7-12.

*Listing 7-12.* Updated Protocol to Handle Deleting Parks and Updating Park List

```
protocol ParkListViewControllerDelegate: class {
    func selectPark(selectedPark: Park?, index: Int) -> Void
    func deletePark(deletedParkIndex: Int) -> Void
}
```

Here we rename the original protocol method, remove the view controller parameter, and add a new index parameter. This will enable us to easily update the user interface after a park has been deleted. Then, we add a new protocol method for deleting a park where we pass in the current park's method.

Next, update the selectPark action to look like Listing 7-13.

*Listing 7-13.* Show Selections of a Park Image

```
@IBAction func selectPark(sender: AnyObject) {
    let selectedRow = sender.selectedRow
    let selectedPark = parks[selectedRow]
    delegate?.selectPark(selectedPark, index: selectedRow)
}
```

Here we create a new constant in which to store the current selected row, update the delegate method call name, and pass in the new index parameter.

Finally, we also need to update the `createPark` action, and this time we only need to change the delegate call to the following:

```
self.delegate?.selectPark(self.parks.last, index: self.parks.endIndex-1)
```

Here we update the name and parameters for the index. We are just using the last index in the parks array, because we simply add new parks to the end of the array.

Now let's update our `MainSplitViewController` to implement the current, updated protocol methods. Open the view controller and update the extension to look like Listing 7-14.

**Listing 7-14.** Implementation of Our Protocol Methods

```
extension MainSplitViewController: ParkListViewControllerDelegate {

    func selectPark(selectedPark: Park?, index: Int) {
        detailViewController.loadPark(selectedPark, index: index)
    }

    func deletePark(deletedParkIndex: Int) {
        masterViewController.deletePark(deletedParkIndex)
    }
}
```

Here we update the `selectPark` method to include the index when calling `loadPark`. This is important for when we need to delete the park and update the Table View of parks. Then we add the new protocol method. This time we are calling a method on the `masterViewController` that will delete the park from the Table View.

Finally, at the end of the `viewDidLoad` method, we set the `detailViewController` delegate to `self`:

```
detailViewController.delegate = self
```

At this point we will have some errors that we will be fixing as we go. Let's move on to updating the detail view controller.

We need to add two new properties–one for storing the park index and the other for storing the delegate (Listing 7-15).

**Listing 7-15.** Updated loadPark Method

```
var parkIndex: Int? = nil
weak var delegate: ParkListViewControllerDelegate? = nil
```

First we need to update the `loadPark` method with two minor changes. Add a new parameter for the index, and then set the local `parkIndex` to that value:

```
func loadPark(park: Park?, index: Int) {
        self.park = park
        self.parkIndex = index
. . . // Rest of the code left out
}
```

Now create a new IBAction called `deletePark` that will call our API, update the detail UI, and call our delegate to `deletePark`, which will remove the park from the list of parks. Create the action with the code in Listing 7-16.

***Listing 7-16.*** New Action for Deleting a Park

```
@IBAction func deletePark(sender: AnyObject) {
    api.deletePark((park?.recordID)!) { [unowned self] (error) -> Void in
        if error != nil {
            print(error!.localizedDescription)
        } else {
            dispatch_async(dispatch_get_main_queue()) {
                self.parkImages.removeAll()
                self.park = nil
                self.delegate?.deletePark(self.parkIndex!)
                self.parkIndex = nil
            }
        }
    }
}
```

Here we call our API deletePark method, passing in the park record ID. If the delete was successful we will have emptied the parkImages array, nil'ed out the park, called the delegate method to delete the park by passing in the park index, and set the parkIndex to nil. We do all this on the main thread. It is important to remember that deleting a Park record type will also delete all the Park Image records that have a reference to it.

Now let's open the Main.storyboard to connect our new delete action. Control-drag from the Delete Park button to the detail view controllers icon, and from the popup select the deletePark action (Figure 7-2).

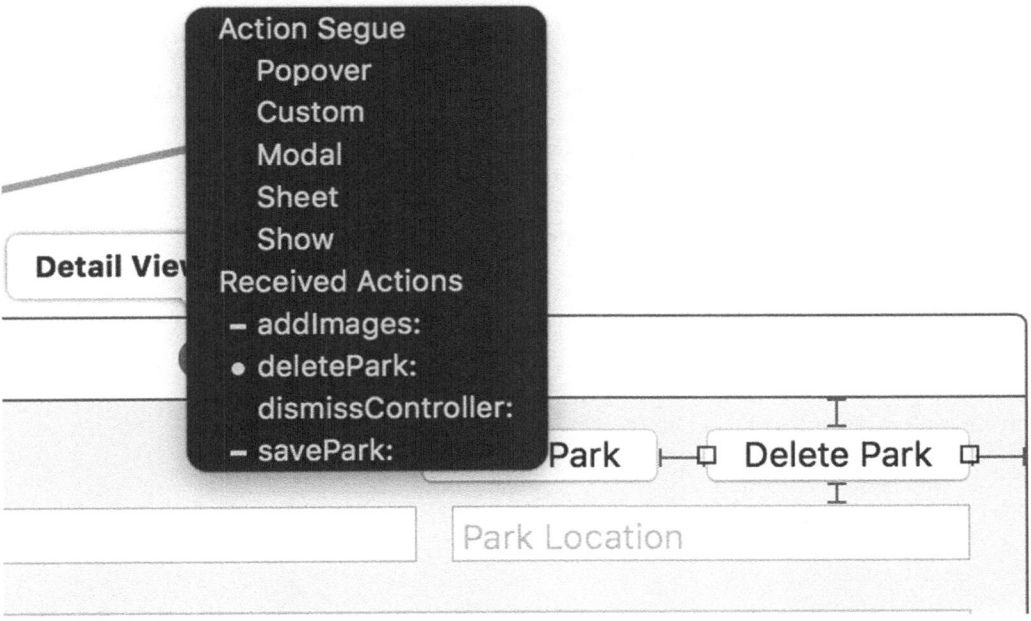

***Figure 7-2.*** *Delete Park button connected to the deletePark action*

Finally, let's go back to our `ParkListViewController` and create the missing `deletePark` function with the code in Listing 7-17.

***Listing 7-17.*** Method That Will Update the Table View to Remove the Deleted Park

```
func deletePark(index: Int) {
    dispatch_async(dispatch_get_main_queue()) {
        self.tableView.deselectRow(index)
        self.tableView.removeRowsAtIndexes(NSIndexSet(index: index), withAnimation:
        NSTableViewAnimationOptions.EffectFade)
        self.parks.removeAtIndex(index)
    }
}
```

Here on the main queue, we first deselect the park we just deleted, then we remove the row where the park was, and finally we remove the park from the parks list.

If you run your app now you should be able to delete an existing park, or create a new park and then delete it. You can also create a park with multiple images, view it in the CloudKit Dashboard, and delete it to ensure all the images related to the park are also deleted.

Now we are able to delete a park along with all the images that belong with it. However, wouldn't it be nice to keep the park and just delete one or more pictures that belong with it? That is exactly what we will do next.

# Deleting Park Images

There are a few minor updates we need to make in order for this to work. First, we need to enable the selection of images in our collection view. Open the `Main.storyboard` using the Document Outliner and find the Park Images Collection in the Detail View Controller scene. Then, in the Attributes Inspector, make sure the checkboxes for "Selectable," "Allows Empty Selection," and "Allows Multiple Selection" are checked. (To select multiple images, hold down the Command key as you select images.)

If we were to run our app and select one or more images we would not see the changes. To fix this we are going to create a subclass of `NSCollectionViewItem` and override the selected property. Create a new Cocoa Class, with subclass `NSCollectionViewItem`, and name it `ParkImageViewItem`. Update the contents of the file so it looks like Listing 7-18.

***Listing 7-18.*** Custom NSCollectionViewItem to Allow Us to Visually Show When an Image Was Selected

```
import Cocoa

class ParkImageViewItem: NSCollectionViewItem {

    override func viewDidLoad() {
        super.viewDidLoad()
        // Do view setup here.
    }
```

```
override var selected: Bool {
    didSet {
        if self.selected {
            self.view.layer?.borderColor = NSColor.orangeColor().CGColor
            self.view.layer?.borderWidth = 3
            self.view.layer?.cornerRadius = 10
        } else {
            self.view.layer?.borderColor = NSColor.clearColor().CGColor
            self.view.layer?.borderWidth = 0
            self.view.layer?.cornerRadius = 0
        }
    }
}
```

Here we use the views layer and set the border color, width, and the corner radius for when the item is selected, and set it so when the item is not selected these changes are not implemented. The selected property is automatically set by Cocoa, so we don't have to worry about manually setting this. We are using the didSet of the computed property so we leave the default behavior intact and only use the updated value for our own purposes.

Finally, we need to update the storyboard to take advantage of our new class. Select the scene that is being used to show an individual image, and then update the custom class in the Identity Inspector to be our new ParkImageViewItem class. Now if you run the app you will be able to see the selected images with an orange outline (Figure 7-3).

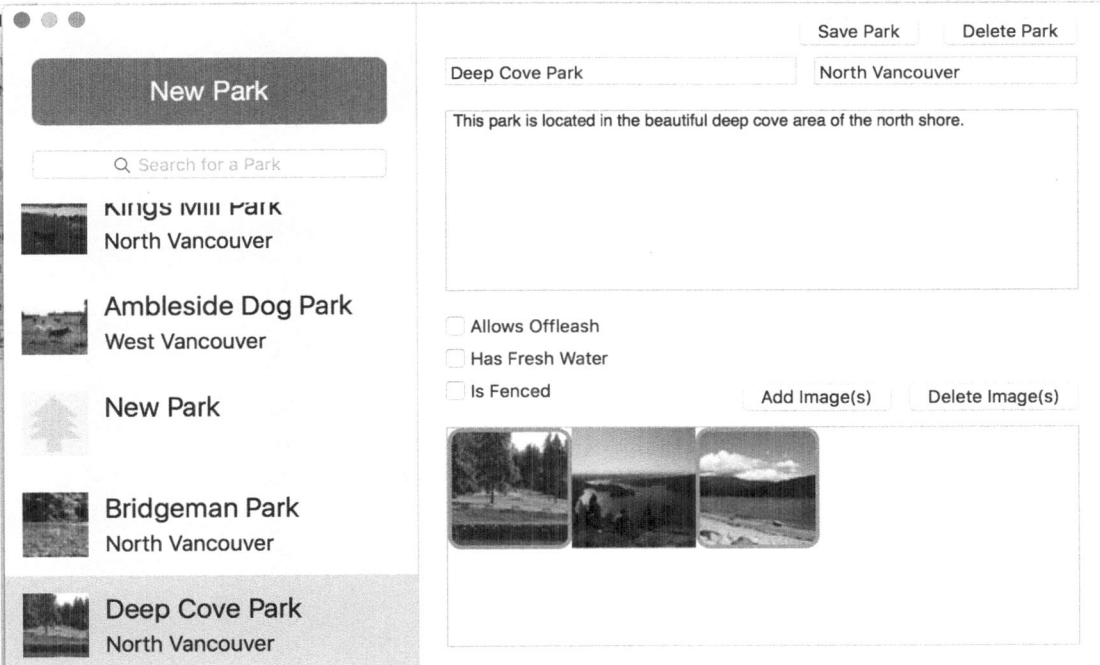

***Figure 7-3.*** *Application running with two selected park images*

We are ready to update our API to handle deleting images. Open the API.swift file and add a new function, as shown in Listing 7-19.

***Listing 7-19.*** API Method That Handles Deleting Park Images

```
func deleteParkImages(imagesToDelete: [ParkImage], completionHandler: NSError? -> Void) {
    var imageRecordIDsToDelete = [CKRecordID]()

    for image in imagesToDelete {
        imageRecordIDsToDelete.append(image.recordID)
    }

    let deleteOperation = CKModifyRecordsOperation(recordsToSave: nil, recordIDsToDelete:
    imageRecordIDsToDelete)
        deleteOperation.atomic = false
        deleteOperation.database = publicDB

        deleteOperation.modifyRecordsCompletionBlock = { (savedRecords: [CKRecord]?,
        deletedRecords: [CKRecordID]?, operationError: NSError?) -> Void in
            completionHandler(operationError)
    }

    NSOperationQueue().addOperation(deleteOperation)
}
```

We want to be able to delete one or more images at the same time, so instead of using the convenience API we use CKModifyRecordsOperation again, but this time instead of passing content to recordsToSave we pass the record IDs we want to delete.

In this function we are passing in an array of ParkImages and a completionHandler that accepts an error or nil. The first thing we need is an array to store the record IDs we want to delete. We then loop through all the image objects we passed into the method to update our IDs array with the image CKRecordID.

Next, we create a CKModifyRecordsOperation to pass nil as the records to save and our array of IDs for the delete parameter. We set atomic to false and tell the operation to use our public database.

Finally, we create a modifyRecordsCompletionBlock that simply calls our completionHandler, passing in any errors that may have occurred. Then we add our operation to the operation queue.

Now let's move back to our DetailViewController to create a new action we will use for deleting images. Create the action in Listing 7-20.

***Listing 7-20.*** Action to Get the Selected Images and Pass Them to deleteParkImages

```
@IBAction func deleteImages(sender: AnyObject) {
    let selectedParkImages = parkImagesCollection.selectionIndexes
    var imagesToDelete: [ParkImage]? = []
    selectedParkImages.enumerateIndexesUsingBlock { [unowned self] (index, _) -> Void in
        imagesToDelete?.append(self.parkImages[index])
    }
    api.deleteParkImages(imagesToDelete!) { (error) -> Void in
        if error != nil {
            print(error!.localizedDescription)
        } else {
            dispatch_async(dispatch_get_main_queue()) {
```

```
            self.imagesArrayController.removeObjectsAtArrangedObjectIndexes
            (selectedParkImages)
        }
      }
    }
}
```

First we need to know which images were selected, so we create a new constant that stores an NSIndexSet of selected images. Then we create an optional array of park images that we want to delete.

We enumerate over the NSIndexSet to get each index and then use that index to update our imagesToDelete array with the image from the parkImages array matching the index.

Once we have the array of images to delete we simply pass it into our api.deleteParkImages call. If there were an error we would print out the error message (in a real-world app you would want to notify the user in some way). If there were no problems deleting the images we would remove the selected indexes from our imagesArrayController on the main thread, which would in turn update our collection view, remove the images, and update the display.

# Make the Search Feature Functional

In this last section we are going to enable the filtering of the results of our park list using the Search field. We are not going to be calling the server to do the filtering; instead, we are only going to be filtering the local copy of parks. It would be a good challenge for you to update the fetchParks API call to actually use the search parameter, then update the NSPredicate to take search terms into consideration and return only parks whose names match the search string.

In order to get the search to work we will need to make some changes to our code. We currently are not using an array controller to handle our parks, but we are going to change our code to use one. This will require a few alterations to the code for selecting and deleting parks.

First, open the Main.storyboard file and drag an array controller onto it. Next, open the Assistant Editor and Control-drag from the array controller to the ParkListViewController file; below the list of outlets create another one called arrayController. Close the Assistant Editor, as we have to make some more changes in the storyboard before moving on.

In the Document Outliner select the Table View, and in the Bindings Inspector update content and selection indexes to look like those in Figure 7-4.

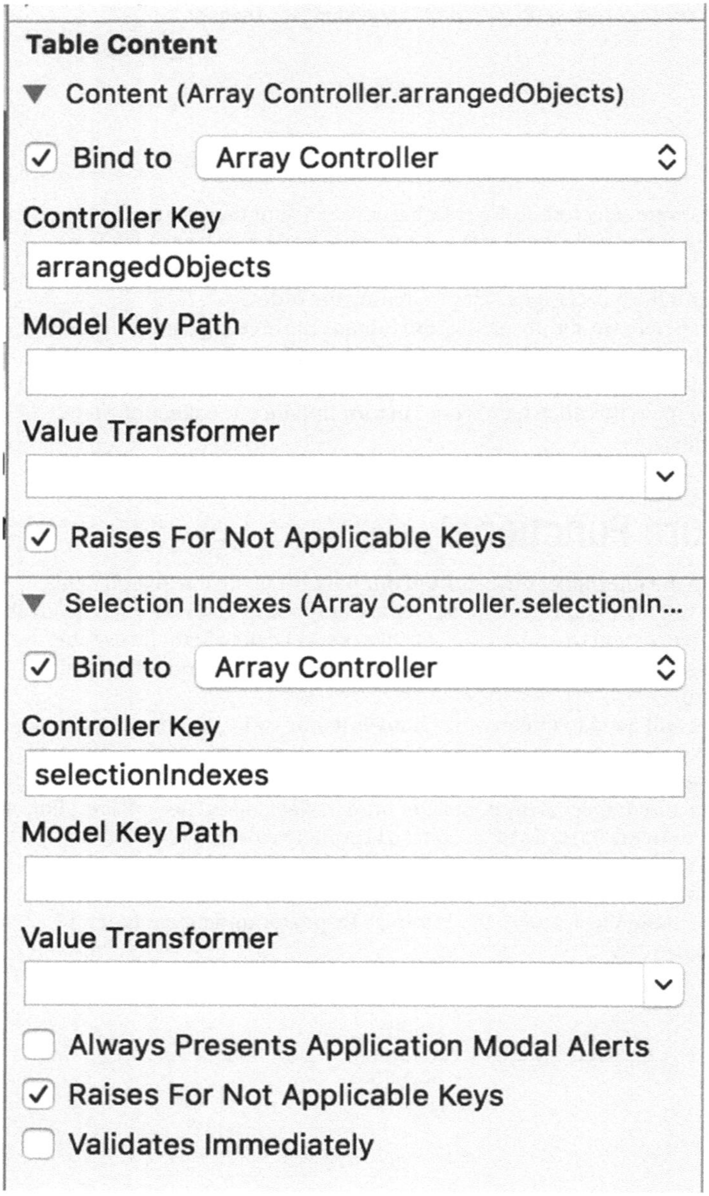

**Table Content**

▼ Content (Array Controller.arrangedObjects)

☑ Bind to [ Array Controller                ⌄ ]

Controller Key

[ arrangedObjects                                 ]

Model Key Path

[                                                 ]

Value Transformer

[                                              ⌄ ]

☑ Raises For Not Applicable Keys

▼ Selection Indexes (Array Controller.selectionIn...

☑ Bind to [ Array Controller                ⌄ ]

Controller Key

[ selectionIndexes                                ]

Model Key Path

[                                                 ]

Value Transformer

[                                              ⌄ ]

☐ Always Presents Application Modal Alerts

☑ Raises For Not Applicable Keys

☐ Validates Immediately

*Figure 7-4. Bindings between the Table View and the Array Controller*

Select the Search field. In the Binding Inspector, bind the search predicate to the array controller, and make sure its Controller Key is set to filterPredicate and the Predicate Format is set to name contains[cd] $value.

Let's open the ParkListViewController to make some code changes. First, update the selectPark action to look like Listing 7-21.

*Listing 7-21.* Updated selectPark to Use the arrayController

```
@IBAction func selectPark(sender: AnyObject) {
        //let selectedRow = sender.selectedRow
        //let selectedPark = parks[selectedRow]
    let selectedRow = arrayController.selectionIndex
    let selectedPark = arrayController.selectedObjects.first as! Park
    delegate?.selectPark(selectedPark, index: selectedRow)
}
```

Now that we are using an `arrayController` we can use it to find the selected index and the selected object. Then we need to update the `deletePark` method to look like Listing 7-22.

*Listing 7-22.* Updated deletePark to Use the New arrayController

```
func deletePark(index: Int) {
    dispatch_async(dispatch_get_main_queue()) {
            self.arrayController.removeObjectAtArrangedObjectIndex(index)
//    self.tableView.deselectRow(index)
//            self.tableView.removeRowsAtIndexes(NSIndexSet(index: index), withAnimation:
            NSTableViewAnimationOptions.EffectFade)
//    self.parks.removeAtIndex(index)
    }
}
```

Here we replace the current lines that update the table list with a single `arrayController` call to `removeObjectAtArrangedObjectIndex`, which we must do since we updated the `select` code to use the array controller's selected row. We don't have to update anything else. When running the app now you should be able to filter the park list results by typing in the Search field, and be able to select or delete a park as before. However, if you are filtering parks the table is also updated as expected.

You may have noticed we have no way to update the park thumbnail that is shown in the list. I left this out on purpose as a challenge for you. You now have enough information to handle this on your own. Tip: check in `saveParkImages` to see if the park already has a thumbnail. If it doesn't, create a new thumbnail of the first image and update the park's thumbnail asset with it.

# Conclusion

This chapter has covered a lot of ground. We have learned how to add parks, add park images, delete parks, and delete park images. We also learned how as code progresses you may be required to make changes to the original design. Finally, we learned how to add and delete multiple records at once.

In the next chapter we will look at some optimizations to improve performance.

■ ■ ■

# CHAPTER 8

# Adding Local Cache to Improve Performance

At this point we have an almost fully functional app. I say "almost" because I left you with a few challenges to complete yourself to finish this app. Your challenges include creating the default thumbnail for the park and loading the full-size image when someone double-clicks on the park image. Apple has an example that will show you exactly how to do this using the Collection View. Find the sample code: CocoaSlideCollection: Using NSCollectionView on OS X 10.11.

In this chapter we are going to focus more on performance. Currently, every time we run the app there is a short delay when the records are pulled from CloudKit, or when we select a park and the park images are downloaded. We also are following some not-so-ideal practices; for example, when we are downloading a park we are getting all the properties, including the thumbnail assets, at the same time. Even though we have generated smaller thumbnail assets they still take time to download. Finally, when we download the park images we are not only downloading the thumbnail but also the full-size image, which could be quite large.

## Caching Park Records

We will first start to improve performance by creating a local cache of our parks list. This will allow us to load the cached data when the app starts instead of waiting for the query, which will make the app appear to be faster.

We need to make our Park object conform to NSCoding, so update the Park class to inherit NSCoding:

```
class Park: NSObject, NSCoding {
```

As soon as you do this you will see compiler errors because we still need to implement two required methods to conform to NSCoding, one for encoding the data and the other for decoding the data.

Add the code in Listing 8-1; it decodes the data for creating a new park object.

***Listing 8-1.*** Decode the Park Object

```
required init(coder aDecoder: NSCoder) {
    let recordName = aDecoder.decodeObjectForKey("recordName") as! String
    self.recordID = CKRecordID(recordName: recordName)
    self.name = aDecoder.decodeObjectForKey("name") as! String
    self.overview = aDecoder.decodeObjectForKey("overview") as! String
    self.location = aDecoder.decodeObjectForKey("location") as! String
    self.isFenced = aDecoder.decodeBoolForKey("isFenced")
```

© Bruce Wade 2016
B. Wade, *OS X App Development with CloudKit and Swift*, DOI 10.1007/978-1-4842-1880-8_8

```
    self.hasFreshWater = aDecoder.decodeBoolForKey("hasFreshWater")
    self.allowsOffleash = aDecoder.decodeBoolForKey("allowsOffleash")
    super.init()
}
```

In this method we are using the NSCoder to decode the different keys used to build our class object. The only more-complicated aspect of this function is getting the recordName from the decoder and using that to create a new CKRecordID object. Everything else is self-explanatory; if you have never used NSCoder before refer to Apple's documentation for more information.

The next function will handle encoding our object so it can be saved to disk (Listing 8-2).

***Listing 8-2.*** Encode the Park Object

```
func encodeWithCoder(aCoder: NSCoder) {
    aCoder.encodeObject(recordID.recordName, forKey: "recordName")
    aCoder.encodeObject(name, forKey: "name")
    aCoder.encodeObject(overview, forKey: "overview")
    aCoder.encodeObject(location, forKey: "location")
    aCoder.encodeBool(isFenced, forKey: "isFenced")
    aCoder.encodeBool(hasFreshWater, forKey: "hasFreshWater")
    aCoder.encodeBool(allowsOffleash, forKey: "allowsOffleash")
}
```

This method does the opposite of the previous function. It takes our already created Park object and gets it ready to be saved out as different key values in a saveable way.

Next we need to add a few methods to our ParkListViewController to handle loading and saving our parks to disk. The cache is only going to be loaded on first load and will be updated every time the query to the server has finished returning new data. Let's create a method that will tell our encoder where to save the park list information (Listing 8-3).

***Listing 8-3.*** Determining the Cache Path

```
func cachePath() -> String {
    let paths = NSSearchPathForDirectoriesInDomains(.CachesDirectory, .UserDomainMask, true)
    let path = paths[0].stringByAppendingString("/parks.cache")
    return path
}
```

Here we are saying that we want to add a file called parks.cache inside the user's cache directory for this app.

Next, let's add another function that will be used to actually write our data to disk (Listing 8-4).

***Listing 8-4.*** Save List of Parks to Disk

```
func persist() {
    let data = NSMutableData()
    let archiver = NSKeyedArchiver(forWritingWithMutableData: data)
    archiver.encodeRootObject(parks)
    archiver.finishEncoding()
    data.writeToFile(cachePath(), atomically: true)
}
```

Now that our Park object knows how to encode itself, we simply pass the list of parks into an NSKeyedArchiver to encode it. Once that is done we write the encoded data to our cache directory, saving it into the parks.cache file.

While it is great that we can encode and save the data, we also need a way to load it back from disk. Let's create a function to do this now (Listing 8-5).

***Listing 8-5.*** Load the Parks from Disk

```
func loadCache() {
    let path = cachePath()
    if let data = NSData(contentsOfFile: path) where data.length > 0 {
        let decoder = NSKeyedUnarchiver(forReadingWithData: data)
        let object: AnyObject! = decoder.decodeObject()
        if object != nil {
            dispatch_async(dispatch_get_main_queue(), { [unowned self] () -> Void in
                self.parks = object as! [Park]
            })
        }
    }
}
```

This method checks to see whether we have any data for the parks stored in the cache directory, and if we do our code will use the NSKeyedUnarchiver to try to decode it into an object. If that is successful we then cast the object into an array of Park objects and update our local parks array on the main queue. It is important to use the main queue here as we are using data binding, and as soon as the local parks array changes, our Table View will update. It is also important that we check if the data even exists before we try to decode it, because on the first run of our app there will be no cached data.

We have a few more updates to make before this will work. First let's update the api.fetchParks call inside viewDidLoad. After you set the local parks variable, call the persist function to write the parks to disk so that the next time we load the app we have cached data to use (Listing 8-6).

***Listing 8-6.*** Updated fetchParks API Call to Persist the Parks That Were Returned

```
api.fetchParks { [unowned self] (parks) -> Void in
    dispatch_async(dispatch_get_main_queue()) {
        self.parks = parks
        self.persist()
    }
}
```

Lastly, we need to tell our app to try to load from the cache when we first start the app. The best place to do this is inside the MainSplitViewController. Open that file and, after setting the masterViewController's delegate, call loadCache on the masterViewController inside the viewDidLoad method (Listing 8-7).

***Listing 8-7.*** Updated viewDidLoad to loadCache on Startup

```
override func viewDidLoad() {
    super.viewDidLoad()
    masterViewController.delegate = self
    masterViewController.loadCache()
    detailViewController.delegate = self
}
```

Now you should be able to build and run your app. The first time you do so you will notice a delay. Stop your app and run it again, and you should notice the park list loads instantaneously, aside from the actual park images, which still have a delay before they are loaded. We will work on setting up another cache for the park thumbnail images next.

We need to update how we fetch parks before we look at caching the images; otherwise, we will be performing duplicate queries to the server for the image assets. Unfortunately, in the initial implementation of our fetchParks API we used the convenience API. We are going to have to replace this with a CKQueryOperation, which will enable us to set the desired keys instead of returning the entire record. Using the CKQueryOperation also gives us the ability to implement pagination using cursors. We will cover the cursors being used; however, it is up to you to get paging working if you wish to implement it, which is highly recommended. Replace the fetchParks function in the API class with Listing 8-8.

***Listing 8-8.*** Updated fetchParks Method

```
func fetchParks(completionHandler: [Park] -> Void) {
   let parksPredicate = NSPredicate(value: true)
   let query = CKQuery(recordType: "Parks", predicate: parksPredicate)
   let queryOp = CKQueryOperation(query: query)
   queryOp.desiredKeys = ["name", "location", "overview", "isFenced", "hasFreshWater",
   "allowsOffleash"]
   runOperation(queryOp, completionHandler: completionHandler)
}
```

We have removed the convenience API call and instead created a CKQueryOperation, passing in our query object. We then tell the query operation which record keys we want returned. Finally, we pass our query operation and our completionHandler to a new function, which we are going to implement next. Now add the code from Listing 8-9 below the fetchPark method in the API class.

***Listing 8-9.*** New API Method for Using CKQueryOperation

```
func runOperation(queryOp: CKQueryOperation,completionHandler: [Park] -> Void) {
    queryOp.queryCompletionBlock = { cursor, error in
        if self.isRetryableCKError(error) {
            let userInfo: NSDictionary = (error?.userInfo)!
            if let retryAfter = userInfo[CKErrorRetryAfterKey] as? NSNumber {
                let delay = retryAfter.doubleValue * Double(NSEC_PER_SEC)
                let time = dispatch_time(DISPATCH_TIME_NOW, Int64(delay))
                dispatch_after(time, dispatch_get_main_queue()) {
                    self.runOperation(queryOp, completionHandler: completionHandler)
                }
                return
            }
        }
        self.queryFinished(cursor, error: error, completionHandler: completionHandler)
        if cursor != nil {
            self.queryNextCursor(cursor!, completionHandler: completionHandler)
        } else {
            completionHandler(self.parks)
        }
    }
```

```
        queryOp.recordFetchedBlock = { record in
            self.fetchedPark(record)
        }
        publicDB.addOperation(queryOp)
}
```

This is a big change, so let's go through it carefully. First we create a query completion block for our query operation. This block will take a cursor and an error. If we limit the amount of records a query can return then the cursor will be a non-nil value that can be used to perform the next query (pagination). After our call we pass the error into a new custom function that determines if the error means we should return the query. Create this new function below the last one in the API class (Listing 8-10).

***Listing 8-10.*** Code to Check for Errors and Determine if It Is a Retryable Error

```
private func isRetryableCKError(error: NSError?) -> Bool {
    var isRetryable = false
    if let error = error {
        let isErrorDomain = error.domain == CKErrorDomain
        let errorCode: Int = error.code
        let isUnavailable = errorCode == CKErrorCode.ServiceUnavailable.rawValue
        let isRateLimited = errorCode == CKErrorCode.RequestRateLimited.rawValue
        let errorCodeIsRetryable = isUnavailable || isRateLimited
            isRetryable = isErrorDomain && errorCodeIsRetryable
    }
    return isRetryable
}
```

If we should retry the query, we pull the information we need from the user's info dictionary to calculate the time we must wait before trying to perform the query again. Next we call a new function, passing in our cursor, error, and completionHandler, which handles updating the parks array by passing it to our completion handler. Listing 8-11 is the code for this new function.

***Listing 8-11.*** Code Called When the Query Is Finished

```
func queryFinished(cursor: CKQueryCursor!, error: NSError!, completionHandler: [Park] ->
Void) {
    completionHandler(self.parks)
}
```

Next we check if there is a valid cursor, and if there is it means we still have more parks that we must fetch from the server. We call a new function to handle this. If there are no more parks to fetch we will not call this function (which will always be our case because by limiting our results we are not taking advantage of the cursor). Listing 8-12 is the code for the queryNextCursor function in the API class.

***Listing 8-12.*** Running a New Query If There Are Still Results to Be Fetched

```
func queryNextCursor(cursor: CKQueryCursor,completionHandler: [Park] -> Void) {
    let queryOp = CKQueryOperation(cursor: cursor)
    runOperation(queryOp, completionHandler: completionHandler)
}
```

This function simply creates a new CKQueryOperation using the cursor we passed in, then we call the runOperation again with our new query operation and repeat the process.

After creating our query completion block, we create another block, recordFetchedBlock (we create this block in the runOperation method), which is called whenever there is a new record returned. In this block we are calling another new function, fetchedPark, that will update our parks array. Listing 8-13 provides the new function in the API class.

*Listing 8-13.* Code Called Whenever a New Park Is Fetched; It Updates Our Parks Array

```
func fetchedPark(parkRecord: CKRecord) {
    var index = NSNotFound
    var park: Park!
    var isNewPark = true
    for (idx, value) in self.parks.enumerate() {
        if value.recordID == parkRecord.recordID {
            // Here we could check to see if the park pulled has been updated and update our
                list if needed.
            // This is left for an exercise to the reader.
            index = idx
            park = value
            isNewPark = false
            break
        }
    }
    if index == NSNotFound {
        park = self.convertCKRecordToPark(parkRecord)
        self.parks.append(park)
        index = self.parks.count - 1
    }
}
```

This function loops through the currently existing parks in the array. If the new record matches one in the parks array, we break out of the loop. Note that we are currently not using this data to update an existing park, but we definitely should. Now if the new park doesn't already exist in the list we convert the record into a park and append it to the parks array, then we set up the next index. We are currently not using the index. However, if you implement pagination you would use this to pass to a new function. This new function would handle inserting the park into the correct index in the array controller that is used in the Table View. In our case we just always return the entire parks array to the completion handler, so we don't need it in our example app as it stands.

We add the operation to our public database. If you run the app again it will run exactly as it did before; however, now we are limiting our results to only the record keys we have queried for. This also means that the thumbnail will now always be the default thumbnail. Before we move on to loading and caching the thumbnail, let's update the convertCKRecordToPark function. In the code that creates a Park instance, remove the parameter that sets the thumbnail, as well as the first few lines in the method that checks for the thumbnail asset (which we will not have any longer).

Finally, to fix the compiler error, update the Park init method to look like Listing 8-14.

**Listing 8-14.** Updated Park init Method

```
init(recordID: CKRecordID, name: String, overview: String, location: String, isFenced: Bool,
hasFreshWater: Bool, allowsOffleash: Bool) {
    self.recordID = recordID
    self.name = name
    self.overview = overview
    self.location = location
    self.isFenced = isFenced
    self.hasFreshWater = hasFreshWater
    self.allowsOffleash = allowsOffleash
    super.init()
    self.thumbnail = NSImage(named: "DefaultParkIcon")!
}
```

Here we remove the thumbnail parameter and replace the other thumbnail code with code to set the default thumbnail. When running the code again everything should work as before, only this time you will see the default thumbnails for each park.

# Caching and Loading Park Thumbnails

Now we have enough code in place to look at loading and caching the thumbnails. Let's set up our image cache path with the following function and add this to the API.swift file (Listing 8-15).

**Listing 8-15.** Code to Determine the Thumbnail Cache Path

```
func imageCachePath(recordID: CKRecordID) -> String {
    let paths = NSSearchPathForDirectoriesInDomains(.CachesDirectory, .UserDomainMask, true)
    let path = paths[0].stringByAppendingString("/\(recordID.recordName)")
    return path
}
```

Here we are using the park's recordID record name–which we pass into this method–as the file name. Let's now create a new function that will either load the cached thumbnail or query the server for the thumbnail and then cache it locally. Listing 8-16 shows the code that also appears in the API.swift file.

**Listing 8-16.** Either Load a Cached Thumbnail or Query CloudKit for One

```
func loadParkThumbnail(parkRecordID: CKRecordID, completion: (photo: NSImage!) -> Void) {
    let backgroundQueue = dispatch_get_global_queue(DISPATCH_QUEUE_PRIORITY_BACKGROUND, 0)

dispatch_async(backgroundQueue) { () -> Void in
        let imagePath = self.imageCachePath(parkRecordID)
        if NSFileManager.defaultManager().fileExistsAtPath(imagePath) {
            let image = NSImage(contentsOfFile: imagePath)
            completion(photo: image)
        } else {
            let fetchOp = CKFetchRecordsOperation(recordIDs: [parkRecordID])
            fetchOp.desiredKeys = ["thumbnail"]
            fetchOp.fetchRecordsCompletionBlock = {
                records, error in
```

```
                self.processThumbnailAsset(parkRecordID, records: records, error: error,
                completionHandler: completion)
            }
            self.publicDB.addOperation(fetchOp)
        }
    }
}
```

We create a background queue to use as we are working with the image. On the background thread, we get the `imagePath` from the image cache for the current park record ID. With this image path, we use the file manager to check if the file exists. If it does exist we use this file and pass it to the completion handler. If the file does not exist we create a new `CKFetchRecordsOperation` using the `parkRecordID` and we fetch the thumbnail field. We create a completion block for the returned record and call a new function that processes the thumbnail asset. Finally, we add the operation to our public database.

Now let's look at the `processThumbnailAsset` function, which downloads the asset and saves it into cache for the next time the app loads (Listing 8-17).

***Listing 8-17.*** Download a Thumbnail Asset and Save It to Cache

```
func processThumbnailAsset(parkRecordID: CKRecordID, records: [NSObject: AnyObject]!, error:
NSError!, completionHandler:(thumbnail: NSImage!) -> Void) {
    if error != nil {
        completionHandler(thumbnail: nil)
    }
    let updatedRecord = records[parkRecordID] as! CKRecord
    if let asset = updatedRecord.objectForKey("thumbnail") as? CKAsset {
        let url = asset.fileURL
        let thumbnail = NSImage(contentsOfFile: url.path!)
        do {
            try NSFileManager.defaultManager().copyItemAtPath(url.path!, toPath:
            imageCachePath(parkRecordID))
        } catch {
          print("There was an issue copying the image")
        }
        completionHandler(thumbnail: thumbnail)
    } else {
        completionHandler(thumbnail: nil)
    }
}
```

If there is an error we pass `nil` to the completion handler; otherwise, we use the park record ID to get the CKRecord out of the returned results. Next we check if the record has a thumbnail asset, and if it does we load the thumbnail and then try to copy the file to our `imageCachePath`. This can fail if the file already exists. Finally, we pass the completion handler our new thumbnail.

Now let's move our focus over to the `ParkListViewController` and create a new function called `LoadThumbnails`. This function will loop though all the parks and call our new `loadParkThumbnail` API call, passing in the park `recordID`. We update the target park's thumbnail on the main thread via the completion handler if there was a photo returned and then reload the table data (Listing 8-18).

***Listing 8-18.*** Load the Thumbnail Images for a Selected Park

```
func loadThumbnails() {
    for (index, park) in self.parks.enumerate() {
        api.loadParkThumbnail(park.recordID) { (photo) -> Void in
            dispatch_async(dispatch_get_main_queue()) {
                if photo != nil {
                    self.parks[index].thumbnail = photo
                    self.tableView.reloadDataForRowIndexes(NSIndexSet(index: index),
                    columnIndexes: NSIndexSet(index: 0))
                }
            }
        }
    }
}
```

Finally, we need to update the `api.fetchParks` completion block to call our `loadThumbnails` function (Listing 8-19).

***Listing 8-19.*** Updated fetchParks API Call to Load Thumbnails

```
api.fetchParks { [unowned self] (parks) -> Void in
    dispatch_async(dispatch_get_main_queue()) {
        self.parks = parks
        self.loadThumbnails()
        self.persist()
    }
}
```

If you run the app you will still notice a little delay, so also update the `loadCache` method so as to call the same `loadThumbnails` inside the `dispatch_async` after we set the park's variable (Listing 8-20).

***Listing 8-20.*** Updated loadCache Method to Also Load Thumbnails

```
func loadCache() {
    let path = cachePath()
    if let data = NSData(contentsOfFile: path) where data.length > 0 {
        let decoder = NSKeyedUnarchiver(forReadingWithData: data)
        let object: AnyObject! = decoder.decodeObject()
        if object != nil {
            dispatch_async(dispatch_get_main_queue(), { [unowned self]() -> Void in
                self.parks = object as! [Park]
                self.loadThumbnails()
            })
        }
    }
}
```

Now if you rerun the app you will see an instant update.

# Caching the Park Images

At this point you should know how to implement caching for the park images. So instead of walking you step by step through it, I will leave you with some pointers on how to accomplish it on your own. I always find that I learn the most when I am forced to implement something myself.

First, you will have to create a cache path, and because record IDs are always unique, you can use the record ID for each of the park images. If you want to take it a step further, you can create a directory using the park record ID as the name and store all the park images in that folder. Remember that we can delete park images, so you are going to want to remove any park images from the cache so they aren't loaded on the reload.

You are also going to want to update the query so it only returns the thumbnail instead of both the thumbnail and the full-size image. This is going to require you to replace the convenience API in the fetchParkImages function. This will give you an opportunity to make some of the functions we created in the last section more generic so you can reuse them in this section.

# Additional Suggested Updates

Wouldn't it be nice to allow users to post comments on different parks? It would be a nice challenge for you to create a new record type for notes that uses the park as a reference. The query for notes is going to be very similar to the park images.

What about adding additional information to the park, like park hours and the actual GPS coordinates for the park, which could then be used to plot the parks on a map?

# Conclusion

This chapter covered a lot of ground and required us to part ways with the convenience API so we could have more control over the data we get from the server. We learned a way to cache objects and images. We learned how to load cached data, making our app more responsive and seem more like it has an instantaneous load, instead of feeling the delay when the app first loads.

This brings us to the end of the book. Feel free to submit pull requests at https://github.com/warplydesigned/DogParksOSX for any new features you have added and want to share with others who have also been working on this app.

# Index

© Bruce Wade 2016
B. Wade, *OS X App Development with CloudKit and Swift*, DOI 10.1007/978-1-4842-1880-8

## ■ T

Thumbnail assets, 89

## ■ U, V

Update DetailViewController, 93
User accounts, 68
User records, 72

## ■ W

Web-based dashboard
        interface, 1

## ■ X, Y, Z

Xcode, 3

# Get the eBook for only $5!

Why limit yourself?

Now you can take the weightless companion with you wherever you go and access your content on your PC, phone, tablet, or reader.

Since you've purchased this print book, we're happy to offer you the eBook in all 3 formats for just $5.

Convenient and fully searchable, the PDF version enables you to easily find and copy code—or perform examples by quickly toggling between instructions and applications. The MOBI format is ideal for your Kindle, while the ePUB can be utilized on a variety of mobile devices.

To learn more, go to www.apress.com/companion or contact support@apress.com.

**Apress®**
THE EXPERT'S VOICE™